The ADHD Parenting Guide for Girls

From Toddlers to Teens Discover How to Respond Appropriately to Different Behavioral Situations

Richard Bass

2 FREE Bonuses!

Receive a FREE <u>Planner for Kids</u> and a copy of the <u>Positive Discipline Playbook</u> by scanning below!

Table of Contents

Interested in listening to the audio version while reading the book? Scan the code below to get a free audio version of The ADHD Parenting Guide for Girls.

Introduction

Picture a room with 1,000 TVs with each TV showing something different. Now try and concentrate on just one TV without getting distracted. –Damian DaViking Aird

ADHD—perhaps one of the most misunderstood mental health disorders—affects almost 10% of children aged 3–17 years in the US (CDC, 2021).

Most of the confusion surrounding ADHD comes from the outside, as many people confuse this neurodevelopmental disorder as being a mere behavioral issue. However, even amongst children living with this condition, those who display subtle, less typical symptoms are often misdiagnosed, or left untreated.

According to the CDC, boys (13%) are twice as likely to get diagnosed with ADHD than girls (6%) (CDC, 2021). The reason for this is that the condition presents itself differently in girls, making it less visible.

What the media often characterizes as ADHD is impulsivity and hyperactivity. However, this is only one type or category of the disorder. The second type or category is inattentiveness, which includes a range of symptoms like difficulty paying attention, inability to complete tasks, and trouble following directions. The third is a combination of both impulsivity/hyperactivity and inattentiveness.

Girl children living with ADHD tend to exhibit the second type or category of the disorder. Since the underlying symptoms are internal and less disruptive, they are either overlooked or misdiagnosed. Instead of being labeled as the stereotypical child who "acts up," girl children with ADHD are commonly seen as lazy, absent-minded, anxious, or perfectionists.

The purpose of this guide is to raise awareness about the invisible symptoms of ADHD that affect girls aged 3–17 years old. In doing so, the intention is to show parents and caregivers how to adapt their approaches to nurturing, communication, and discipline to support their children's development at different ages.

Over the span of ten chapters, parents and caregivers will be given a range of tools and strategies, specifically curated to support highly sensitive and often distracted girl children with ADHD.

They will walk away with more insight into the secret lives of their children and the best parenting approaches to use when seeking to strengthen the parent-child bond.

Chapter 1:

The World Behind the Pretty

Smile

I am not absentminded. It is the presence of mind that makes me unaware of everything else. –G.K. Chesterton

Yes, ADHD Does Affect Girls

It is common for people to associate ADHD with young boys, and quite frankly, this is an honest mistake. The "face" of ADHD is typically a hyperactive five-year-old boy, who fidgets in class, gets lost in the supermarket, and struggles to regulate their emotions.

But the truth is that ADHD can present itself in more ways than one—*and in girls, just as much as boys.*

There are three types or categories of ADHD:

- Impulsive and hyperactive

- Inattentive

- Combination of both

When diagnosing the disorder, doctors examine whether a child displays at least one of these types or categories on an ongoing basis. Research shows that young boys are twice as likely to receive a diagnosis due to displaying impulsive and hyperactive behaviors that are more noticeable and disruptive in daily life. Young girls, on the other hand, tend to display inattentive behaviors, which are often missed or misdiagnosed as something else.

Girl children with ADHD have also been found to develop compensatory adaptive behaviors that disguise their symptoms. For example, a young girl might procrastinate or become frustrated whenever it is time to sit down and complete their homework. This avoidant behavior is a cover-up for their inability to maintain focus on what feels to them like a mentally demanding task.

Other children, especially older girls, might develop harmful compensatory adaptive behaviors, such as lying to get out of performing certain tasks, hiding important belongings like school papers, or avoiding/making excuses not to attend social interactions with others, as a way to cope with the anxiety caused by their hidden symptoms.

If you are not aware of the inattentive type of ADHD, you can mistakenly believe that your child is careless, forgetful, defiant, or too emotional. It is therefore important to explore what exactly inattentiveness looks like, so you can provide the necessary support for your children as soon as possible.

Common Symptoms of Inattentiveness

ADHD and learning disabilities go hand-in-hand, and oftentimes children receive a diagnosis after a learning disability is suspected. For instance, a child who has trouble staying organized or paying attention in class might be recommended by their schoolteacher for medical evaluation. But since girls do not fit the mental picture of a typical child with ADHD, their learning disabilities may go undetected.

One of the predictors of ADHD in girls is inattentiveness. Parents may be able to identify inattentiveness at home when their children engage in tasks that require mental effort, such as doing household chores, completing homework, or following directions. Schoolteachers may be able to identify inattentiveness when students fail to meet deadlines, forget material they have just read, or frequently appear to be daydreaming during class.

The diagnostic and statistical manual of mental health disorders (DSM-5) mentions nine symptoms related to inattentive ADHD. In order to receive a diagnosis, doctors look for at least six of these symptoms in children under 17 years old, which must be present for a long period of time and interfere with the child's daily functioning.

The nine symptoms of inattentiveness that you can look out for in your child include:

1. Missing the details

Your child may struggle to pay close attention to details or make what would seem to be "careless" mistakes. When completing homework, for example, they may rush through the assignment, forgetting vital steps along the way.

2. Short attention span

Your child may have trouble maintaining focus on a single task or activity. This may result in half-completed work, abandoned chores, or complaining during long activities that require concentration.

3. Poor listening skills

Your child may appear to not be listening, even when they are spoken to directly. For instance, they might get half of the instructions to complete an exercise, and not hear the rest. Another sign of poor listening skills is interrupting others while they speak, forgetting the names of people or locations, or appearing to zone out during a conversation.

4. Lack of follow through

Your child may struggle to follow instructions that involve multiple steps, like household chores or homework assignments (e.g., they may forget methods or processes involved in completing tasks). The lack of follow-through may result in poorly executed tasks, like putting laundry inside a washing machine, but forgetting to put the machine on.

5. Disorganized

Your child may find it difficult to stay organized or keep track of daily tasks and deadlines. For example, they may remember to complete an assignment the day before it is due, or they can misplace belongings in a cluttered bedroom or workspace.

6. Apathy toward tasks

Due to their inability to maintain focus on tasks, your child may outright refuse to complete them. For example, they might drag their feet whenever they have to study for an upcoming exam, or become frustrated when reminded to do chores. This behavior can be confused as laziness or defiance.

7. Losing or misplacing essential items

Your child may frequently misplace materials that are required to complete essential everyday tasks. For example, they may forget where they placed their backpack or mobile phone. At times, they may need to be reminded to pack essential items, like books, school lunches, or sports equipment, otherwise, they may leave the house without them.

8. Forgetfulness

Your child may forget to complete routine daily tasks and activities. This is often due to other symptoms like the inability to follow through, not paying attention to details, and trouble staying organized. As your child gets older, their forgetfulness can come across as rude (i.e., when they forget to follow instructions) or careless (i.e., when they forget about an assignment deadline).

9. Easily distracted

Lastly, your child can be easily distracted by sounds, objects, or activity in their environment. In class, they may often be seen staring out of a window or doodling in their notebook. Their distractibility can be confused as being disinterested in the task at hand.

You may be reading through these symptoms and recognizing some of them in your boy child with ADHD. Inattentive ADHD is not exclusive to girl children, similar to how hyperactive ADHD is not exclusive to boy children. Nevertheless, these symptoms are more likely to be exhibited by girl children, or children who display a combination of both types.

The Risk of Missed Symptoms

Due to the gendered nature of ADHD, early signs and symptoms can be missed or misdiagnosed in girls. This puts girls at risk of developing maladaptive coping mechanisms to cope with their condition.

For example, to compensate for being disorganized and forgetting about an assignment due in the morning, a teenage girl with ADHD might frantically stay up the whole night completing their assignment. Or to avoid missing important information, like detailed instructions, they might develop perfectionist tendencies and go excessively overboard with doing things right.

Young girls who aren't diagnosed may also experience low self-esteem as a result of their symptoms. This is mostly caused by stereotypes perpetuated in culture, such as a girl must be smart, polite, and organized. Schoolteachers may unknowingly reinforce these stereotypes by overlooking a boy student's disorganization or poor academic performance while enforcing stronger measures to discipline or correct the same symptoms in a girl student.

The risks of missed symptoms extend outside the classroom and affect social interactions too. Research has shown that girls with ADHD are more likely to face rejection than boys. This has to do with the cultural expectation for girls to be more socially conscious, cooperative, and capable of building and maintaining friendships. Since inattentive ADHD causes girls to be poor listeners and struggle to pick up on social cues, they may find it harder to socialize or intuitively respond to the needs of others.

Another common occurrence in girls with ADHD is misdiagnosis. Parents, doctors, and teachers may be able to tell that something is wrong but struggle to identify that "something" as inattentive ADHD. Instead, they might pick up on co-existing mental health disorders, such as mood, sleep, and eating disorders.

For instance, a survey found that girls with ADHD were three times more likely than boys to be prescribed antidepressants before receiving a diagnosis (Connolly, 2022). Due to hiding their symptoms and constantly comparing themselves to non-ADHD girls, they can suffer from stress, anxiety, and depression. Some of the frequent thoughts that might cross their minds are:

- "I need to work harder than everyone else."

- "Something is wrong with me."

- "I'm not as smart as other people."

- "This task needs to be done perfectly."

- "Nobody likes me."

The pressure of having to look and function like a normal student or child, while suffering internally, can take a toll on the girls' emotional well-being. But still, seeking treatment for co-existing disorders like anxiety or depression isn't enough to regulate symptoms associated with ADHD, like the inability to concentrate for long periods of time.

Helping Girls With ADHD

The best way to help your girl child with ADHD is to take action as soon as you suspect that something might be wrong. Early behavioral signs to look out for include (but not limited to):

- Trouble keeping up with school assignments and deadlines.

- Tendency to run late even when they are aware of their schedule.

- Appearing to be dazed or daydreaming during conversation or when they are left to complete tasks.

- Forgetting information they have just been told by someone.

Consult a licensed child doctor, such as a pediatrician or occupational therapist, who has received training in childhood behavior and development. They will be able to examine your child and provide a diagnosis, according to the DSM-5 criteria. Once your child has received a diagnosis, they will be given a treatment plan, which may consist of medication, psychotherapy, or both. The type of treatment your child receives will vary depending on their age, medical history, and overall health.

Nurturing the Girl Behind the Pretty Smile

The purpose of this guide is to teach parents how to support their girl children with ADHD. This may or may not be after their children have received a diagnosis. In other words, the tools and strategies you will learn in the following chapters are effectively independent of your treatment plan (or lack thereof).

The main focus will be on addressing the invisible symptoms associated with inattentive ADHD, such as:

- trouble regulating emotions and taking criticism

- frequently dazing off or daydreaming

- inability to manage time and stay organized

- low sense of self-worth

- difficulty building and maintaining friendships

- difficulty following rules and instructions

Knowing how to identify and help your child manage these symptoms can boost their self-confidence, improve their overall well-being, and strengthen your parent-child relationship.

Chapter Takeaways

- ADHD is more likely to be diagnosed in boys than girls. This is often why some regard the condition as a "boy's disorder."

- The reason why the condition is often missed or undiagnosed in girls is due to how it presents itself, showing up as inattentiveness rather than hyperactivity.

- When left undiagnosed, girls may learn to hide their symptoms, which can lead to issues such as low self-esteem, anxiety, depression, perfectionist tendencies, or trouble building and maintaining relationships.

- The purpose of this guide is to help parents recognize these invisible symptoms of ADHD, so they can teach their girl children healthy coping strategies to combat further emotional and mental health issues.

Chapter 2:

Intimacy = In To Me See

Every word, facial expression, gesture, or action on the part of a parent gives the child some message about self-worth. –Virginia Satir

ADHD and Emotional Regulation

Although emotional dysregulation is not listed as one of the symptoms of ADHD in the DSM-5, research shows that 70% of people living with ADHD experience it (Beheshti et al., 2020). This may be due to the fact that ADHD affects how emotions are processed in the brain.

Studies looking at brain images have shown that children with ADHD have trouble registering delayed gratification. When they feel an urge or desire for something, they want it done instantly, and are more likely to feel frustrated when they aren't able to obtain it.

For example, your child may set a standard to achieve 80% on their test. Since more mental effort is required for them to learn and memorize information, they might spend weeks studying and preparing for the test. However, even after their effort, they might only achieve 75% on the test. This can be disappointing for any child, but it is especially difficult for your child to accept. As a parent, you might encourage them to see where they made mistakes and be mindful of them next time, but "next time" doesn't register with your child. Their inability to score 80% on the test is perceived as a failure.

Leading on from this, another interesting fact about ADHD is that it makes it hard for children to differentiate between minor problems and real-life threats. What would ordinarily seem to be a stressful but solvable situation is to them a serious offense that could sabotage the rest of their life.

As a result, your child may be susceptible to irrational fears, particularly concerning their social lives. They may fear that others don't like them, or that they aren't good enough to make friends. If not addressed, these irrational fears can cause social anxiety and make it that much harder for them to develop meaningful relationships with others.

You may have also noticed that your child struggles to cope with intense emotions, like anger, excitability, or sadness. Any emotion that feels "too good" or "too bad" is likely to throw them off balance and cause anxiety. Sometimes, being surprised with good news can elicit the same fear as failing a test or being rejected by others.

The saying, "Going from zero to 100" describes just how quickly your child can be emotionally triggered and overwhelmed by their emotions. When this occurs, it can sometimes feel like nothing that you say can help them see things from a fair and rational point of view.

If you can relate to some of these examples, please know that there isn't anything wrong with your daughter. She simply feels things more deeply than others. To help her manage strong emotions and cope with stressful events, you can help her develop three prosocial emotions that improve emotional regulation.

Three Emotions for Better Emotional Regulation

We can define emotional dysregulation as the inability to pause and examine emotions. When stressful situations arise, the time between feeling a strong emotion and acting upon it is a matter of seconds.

But let's face it, life is stressful, and to prepare your daughter for these emotionally taxing events, you can teach her how to cultivate positive emotions. Research shows that proactive and positive emotions are one of the best ways to reduce troublesome behaviors and increase cooperation. This is in line with the positive parenting approach, where good behaviors are rewarded, and more than bad behaviors are punished.

It is also worth considering how your child can benefit from cultivating positive emotions. In general, children with ADHD experience a hard time managing negative emotions because doing so requires a lot of mental and emotional effort—an exercise that takes a tremendous toll on them, compared to non-ADHD children. It is much easier for them to shift to positive emotions during stressful moments because it requires less effort and feels more rewarding.

An example would be a primary school child who is anxious about making new friends at their new school. Since their ADHD brain is wired to confuse realistic events with imagined events, the young girl might fear being bullied by her peers, even though there isn't any evidence of this. This anxiety might be enough to make her emotional each time she thinks about going to school.

Cultivating proactive and positive emotions might look like this: Instead of telling the little girl that her fears are irrational and nothing bad is going to happen, you can shift her attention away from the stressful thought and onto something positive— like what she is looking forward to at her new school.

You might find that she is looking forward to wearing a brand new uniform, playing on the huge obstacle course on the field, or renting out books from the library. Conversations around these positive outcomes can shift the young girl's perspective about school, and gradually cause her to go from thinking about the worst-case scenario to feeling excited about the upcoming positive changes.

There are three future-focused emotions that are proactive and positive, which can help your daughter become more resilient, and improve their emotional regulation skills. These are gratitude, pride, and compassion. Below is a brief explanation of each and the fun ways that you can introduce them to your child.

Gratitude

Gratitude is the feeling of being thankful for what you have. Its job is to help you recognize the significance of each passing moment and accept it for what it is. Teaching your child gratitude can help them accept current life situations for what they are and stop seeking out the next best thing.

Here are a few ways to teach gratitude:

- Start a family ritual around the dinner table where everyone takes turns mentioning one thing that made them happy or inspired them that day.

- Sit down with your child and create a gratitude jar using an old mason jar and craft supplies. Whenever they behave well, receive a compliment, or complete a mentally draining task, write a note about the accomplishment and place it inside the jar. Whenever your child needs motivation to keep going, encourage them to read the notes inside the jar.

- Encourage your child to say "thank you" whenever a friend, family member, or schoolteacher performs a duty that makes their lives better. For example, they can thank mom for cooking dinner, thank their sibling for sharing toys, and thank their schoolteacher for the lesson.

- Hang up a support board somewhere in the house where anyone can pin "support requests" related to tasks that other family members can assist them with. The pinned requests should leave enough space for the "helpers" to write their names on them so that it is public for everyone to see how they are being supported by one another.

Pride

Pride can be both a positive and negative emotion. When it is positive, it increases your sense of self-worth, promotes self-control, and pushes you to continue striving to be the best you can be. Teaching your daughter to take pride in who they are and what they are capable of doing will improve their stress tolerance and motivation.

Below are a few strategies that can instill a sense of pride:

- Find a skill that your child enjoys and is good at, and create more opportunities for them to practice it. For example, if they enjoy and are good at cooking, make time over the weekends to prepare a recipe together, or help them bake cupcakes for their class. Let them feel like an expert too, by allowing them to take the lead.

- Catch your child performing behavior that makes you happy and mention how proud you are of them. You might say, "I noticed that you cleaned out your plate before dropping them inside the sink. That made me really happy. Good job!"

- Assign your child responsibilities around the house. Discuss with them what contribution they would like to make toward keeping the household functioning. For younger kids, you may want to give them three age-appropriate tasks to choose from. Give them flexibility on how and when to perform the task (i.e., after playtime, or on the weekends).

Compassion

Compassion is the feeling of concern or empathy toward oneself or others. Teaching your child how to be compassionate can reduce self-centeredness and help them understand that they are a part of a greater ecosystem of people, who may very well be going through the same challenges they are also experiencing. A compassionate child is more likely to be patient and cooperative during difficult times.

Here are a few strategies to teach compassion:

- Promote the message that your family is a team and share similar interests, goals, and even obstacles. Reinforce the concept of being a team by spending quality time together, creating family rules, establishing rituals, and supporting one another.

- Set up monthly dates with your child, where you spend quality time together and bond over an activity you both love. Use these opportunities to find out what is happening in your child's life, and look for ways that you can support them.

- Talk openly about your child's ADHD with them, and other family members, so that they can understand some of their unique strengths and challenges. Show openness to answering your child's questions and exploring treatment options that they might suggest. The greater their insight into ADHD and the associated symptoms, the more self-aware and grounded they will be.

These are just a few strategies to get you started. Experiment with different ways of incorporating gratitude, pride, and compassion into your child's daily life. Moreover, learn to cultivate these proactive and positive emotions in yourself, so that you can model healthy coping behaviors during stressful times.

What Is Emotional Safety?

Physical safety is one of the primary needs of all children. To feel physically safe, they need a roof over their heads, three daily meals, water to drink, and clothes on their backs.

But that isn't where safety starts and ends. Parents and caregivers have the responsibility to make children feel emotionally safe too, which involves creating an environment that allows children to feel comfortable expressing thoughts and emotions (whether appropriate or inappropriate), without feeling judged or rejected.

A warm meal and cozy house won't make children feel emotionally safe. Food and shelter are examples of physical needs that provide a sense of physical security but do little to protect children's psychological needs. Furthermore, parents and caregivers are unable to make their children feel emotionally safe since the feeling comes from within. They can only create an environment for their children to explore who they are, and what they think and feel.

A common concern for parents of girls with ADHD is that they cannot get their daughters to open up about their feelings, or how living with ADHD affects them. Many times, girls develop masking behaviors that disguise symptoms of ADHD or the emotional impact of the pressures imposed on them. It can be difficult to get a young girl, especially during the pre-teen and teenage years, to show vulnerability and share their fears, insecurities, and learning challenges with their parents.

If you struggle to get your child to open up about their feelings, why not consider different ways to create an emotionally safe environment? Or at least improve the emotionally safe environment that already exists? This won't guarantee that your daughter will start sharing their thoughts and feelings, but it will make it easier if they decide to.

How to Become an "Emotionally Safe" Person for Your Child

Getting a child to talk freely about what they are going through is every parent's wish. While it is necessary during the early childhood years, it starts to matter more when the child becomes more independent and a natural rift starts forming between them and their parents.

As a parent, you might be asking yourself: *How do I create an emotionally safe environment for my child?* The answer to this question is being an emotionally safe person for your child.

Think about a time when you were around someone and felt like you were walking on eggshells. In their presence, you didn't feel safe voicing your opinions, in case they unexpectedly triggered a strong emotional reaction from the other person. The only amount of "opening up" you felt comfortable doing was engaging in the occasional small talk—nothing more!

Or how about a time when you were around someone who you felt criticized everything you did? It seemed to you that nothing you did was ever good enough. Whenever you would try to open up, they would remind you of past mistakes, look for details to nitpick, or find ways to redirect the conversation to them in an attempt to upstage you or steal your spotlight.

Being around people like that didn't make you feel emotionally safe. The last thing you wanted to do was show vulnerability because you didn't trust that it would be received with unconditional love and acceptance. The less they knew about you, or what you were up to, the better!

Being an emotionally safe person for your child is about being mindful of how you impact their lives. Think about how your child feels in your presence, or how they respond to you during conversations. Do they seem closed off, afraid to speak or disagree, or uncomfortable? Or do they smile, make eye contact, and provide their own thoughts and feelings about various topics?

The level of openness, compassion, and acceptance you have toward yourself will be reflected in the amount of openness, compassion, and acceptance you bring into the parent-child relationship. You cannot change your child and make them feel what they are not ready to feel; however, you can start to improve the relationship you have with yourself so that you can be emotionally available and "safe" for your child.

Below are a few reflection questions about your journey as a parent thus far, and past experiences that may or may not affect how emotionally safe you are toward your child. Take time to reflect on your answers. Note that you don't need to answer all of the questions.

1. What was it like growing up in your family? Write down a few keywords/adjectives to describe your upbringing.

   _____

   _____

   _____

   _____

2. Describe the relationship you had with your parents. Are there parenting behaviors you saw back then that you have carried over in raising your child?

   _____

   _____

   _____

   _____

3. Did you find it easy to share your thoughts and feelings with your parents? Why or why not?

   _____

_____

_____

_____

4. As an adult, how do you cope with life's challenges? Provide a list of coping strategies or beliefs that get you through hard times.

_____

_____

_____

_____

5. How do you expect your child to cope with life's challenges? Do you tend to expect them to respond the same way you do?

_____

_____

_____

_____

6. How have your childhood experiences influenced the relationship with your child? Mention positive and harmful ways that your past affects your parenting.

_____

7. Now that you understand what being an emotionally safe person means, how can you bring more openness, compassion, and acceptance into your parent-child relationship?

Habits to Cultivate Emotional Safety

Becoming an emotionally safe person is an inside job. But there are a few healthy relationship habits that you can start practicing building trust, show more acceptance, and be more emotionally available for your child. These habits include:

- **Be accepting of all feelings, even those that you don't share or understand.** There are hundreds of emotions, categorized as primary and secondary emotions. Be mindful that at any moment, your child can express feeling something you have never felt or recognized before. Instead of dismissing their feelings, show curiosity by learning more about their experience, how it feels in their body, and the impact it has on their lives.

- **Encourage sitting with strong emotions.** As a parent, your initial response to an emotional child is to fix their problems or tell them that everything will be okay. However, sometimes, this behavior can be invalidating. Your child may just want someone to listen to or mirror what they are feeling. Take time out to just sit with your child and allow them to vent or say whatever is on their minds, without going into problem-solving mode.

- **Empathize and validate your child's emotions.** Take a moment to picture what your child may be going through. Imagine how what they are going through can feel stressful or confusing for someone their age. Validate their experience by acknowledging that it is real and impactful in their lives. You might say, "What you are feeling makes sense" or "I can imagine how upset you felt when that happened."

- **Promote the message that it's okay to have bad days.** Express to your child that feeling negative emotions is normal and nothing to be ashamed about. They don't need to feel pressure to always be positive because life isn't always positive. Whenever they might be feeling down, reassure them that it is okay to have bad days and soon those emotions will pass.

- **Be open and available to talk about anything—including those awkward topics.** You were once a curious young girl or teenager who had so many questions about the world and needed someone to provide emotional support and guidance. You have the opportunity to be that person for your child, by letting your guard down and being open to having tough conversations with them. Let them know that nothing is off-limits, and you will try to provide the best possible answer that won't cause further confusion.

- **Be aware of your own projections.** Through practices like mindfulness, you are able to gain a deeper awareness of your own thoughts, beliefs, emotions, and traumas. During interactions with your child, you can practice separating what you think and feel from what is actually taking place in the moment. Not only will this prevent you from being triggered, but it will also make your child more comfortable expressing who they are, without feeling judged.

These habits will help you build or strengthen the foundation of trust between you and your child. This type of safe relationship can inspire your child to open up more about what they are thinking and feeling. Remember, all you can do as a parent is create an emotionally safe environment. The decision to connect and show vulnerability is your child's to make.

Chapter Takeaways

- ADHD affects intimacy in close relationships, particularly the parent-child relationship, due to symptoms like poor emotional regulation.

- Children with ADHD have a hard time regulating their emotions, even though this symptom is not listed under the DSM-5 criteria for ADHD diagnosis.

- Signs of emotional dysregulation can include low resilience, inability to restore balance after a stressful situation, or persistently experiencing negative emotions. When these symptoms aren't addressed, they can lead to various mood disorders.

- Teaching your daughter how to regulate their emotions is about emphasizing proactive and positive emotions, rather than trying to control negative emotions. Three future-based proactive and positive emotions to cultivate in your child are gratitude, pride, and compassion.

- Creating or strengthening emotional safety in your parent-child relationship can also encourage your child to share their thoughts and feelings. Emotional safety is created when your child feels comfortable being themselves around you, without feeling judged.

- Being an emotionally safe parent is an inside job. It begins by deepening openness, compassion, and acceptance toward yourself.

In the final chapter, you will find various emotional regulation exercises and prompts that can improve your child's emotional regulation skills.

Chapter 3:

Alternatives to "NO!"

If a child can't learn the way we teach, maybe we should teach the way they learn. –Ignacio Estrada

Understanding Your Child's Sensitivity to Criticism

Parenting a child with ADHD, who may not listen the first time you give an instruction, or who gets easily distracted by gadgets or TV, can be frustrating! Even at school, your child's teachers may get irritated by having to constantly remind them to focus on the task at hand and quit doodling or looking out the window.

Improper behaviors, like not paying attention, following instructions, or working diligently on tasks such as homework are not acceptable. However, what does this mean for a young girl who is more likely to get caught behaving improperly due to learning and social challenges?

William Dodson, a clinician, and expert on ADHD treatment argues that children with ADHD receive more negative or correct comments from parents and teachers than non-ADHD children. In fact, at school alone, Dodson believes that students with ADHD will receive 20,000 more negative or correct comments by the time they turn 10, than non-ADHD students (Frye, 2020).

It is understandable why children with ADHD who may display disruptive or inappropriate behaviors would receive a disproportionate amount of criticism. However, what tends to be overlooked is how constantly being criticized affects children.

A study conducted by a research team at Okinawa Institute of Science and Technology Graduate University wanted to find out how children with ADHD respond to rewards and punishment compared to non-ADHD children. They observed 210 children, 145 of them who were diagnosed with ADHD, and asked them to play two different computer games.

Both games could result in one of three outcomes: winning, losing, or neutral. The games provided children with equal opportunities for winning and deducted the same number of points for losses. The difference though was that one game was designed to have an increased chance of losing. Plus, every time a player lost, they would hear a sound that was akin to mocking laughter (Furukawa et al., 2016).

Children were given the choice to play both games, until they reached a certain number of points, or completed 300 turns. Within the first 100 turns, both groups of children started out with the favorable game (the one which was less punishing). In the next 100 turns, children with ADHD remained committed to the less punishing game, while non-ADHD children experimented with the other game.

During the last 100 turns, children with ADHD continued to avoid the punishing game, while the rest were still open to the idea of winning the challenging game. It became clear to the researchers that children with ADHD seem to be more sensitive to punishment than non-ADHD children.

Studies like these can help parents and caregivers understand why their children might respond negatively to certain tasks that could be perceived as "punishing," like completing math homework or doing household chores. The task isn't necessarily what is punishing, but the effort involved in completing the task may be.

For example, a teenage girl with ADHD may find the task of attending a social event punishing because of the amount of communicating, listening, sharing, and networking they may have to do. Similarly, they may find the task of studying for a test punishing because of the excessive amount of information they need to learn and memorize. Essentially, the more effort a task requires, the more incentives the child needs to make it feel less punishing.

Criticism or language perceived as being punishing, like "No" or "You don't listen!" can make it harder for your child to complete tasks that require a lot of effort (i.e., tasks that offer little incentives). It is almost as though you are creating more reasons in your child's head for them to not cooperate with you. Changing your language and using more positive words and body language can increase the perceived rewards of performing demanding tasks, and help your child remain resilient.

The Dangers of Highly Critical Parenting

Overly critical parenting can not only negatively affect your child's self-esteem, but it can also worsen the symptoms of ADHD. A 2016 study found a correlation between ongoing and persistent symptoms of ADHD and high parental criticism. Researchers observed the effects of parental criticism and overprotectiveness on 388 children with ADHD and 127 without ADHD.

Parents were also asked to give two interviews, one year apart. The researchers asked questions related to parenting and rated the use of harsh descriptive words, levels of emotional over-involvement, and levels of negativity.

The findings revealed that children of parents who were more critical of them as people—rather than focusing on or correcting their troublesome behavior—showed severe and persistent symptoms of ADHD by the time they reached their teenage years (Musser et al., 2016). This pattern was more common in children who displayed hyperactive ADHD, as well as those who were diagnosed with other related conditions like oppositional defiant disorder (ODD).

The danger of highly critical parenting is that it makes it harder for children with ADHD to manage, or even reduce the severity of their symptoms. As they grow older, they may become more hyperactive or inattentive, creating a lot of disruptions in their lives and negatively impacting their self-esteem.

Signs You May Be an Overly Critical Parent

There is no such thing as "right" or "wrong" parenting. Nobody receives a handbook at the hospital after their child is born, instructing them on the right way to raise a healthy and confident child. Furthermore, due to each parent's varied life experiences, cultural background, and social conditioning, they might have their own preferences for raising their kid.

Nonetheless, we can identify "helpful" and "harmful" parenting by the approach used to communicate with, and discipline children. Helpful parenting focuses on teaching and guiding children on how to be responsible, socially aware, and confident human beings. Children are not expected to be perfect, demonstrate common sense, or intuitively know how to act in various situations. Instead, parents are the ones who step in and correct behaviors, without attacking their children's self-image.

Harmful parenting does the opposite of this. It focuses on instilling obedience to parents, rather than teaching and guiding children how to be productive human beings. In other words, going against the parents' orders is more of an offense than behaving improperly. Thus, children are more likely to be criticized for who they are, instead of being taught acceptable and unacceptable behaviors.

Overly critical parenting can be harmful to your child's development. What's worse is the harsh behaviors or language you use may be so normalized in your household that you aren't even aware that it is coming across as highly critical, overbearing, or controlling. Below are a few signs that you may be an overly critical parent:

- **You experience frequent mood swings.** The feelings of being on edge stressed, or overwhelmed may follow you throughout the day, making it difficult to overlook typical childish behavior or minor mistakes or inconveniences that your child makes.

- **You tend to mock or use biting humor.** Your eye may be trained to look for problems in how your child looks, walks, talks, or spends their time. Instead of addressing these perceived issues privately or compassionately, you may raise them as a joke or judgmental comment like, "Why do you eat like that?"

- **You are dismissive of your child's feelings.** It can be difficult for you to empathize with your child because you don't see their life struggles as being struggles at all. Perhaps you have been through worse situations and can't wrap your head around why your child would display such huge emotions for something that seems trivial. Without realizing it, you might shrug off your child's feelings or instruct them to toughen up.

- **You tend to be controlling.** You may doubt your child's ability to make decisions on their own. As such, you prefer to control their behaviors, how they spend their time, where they go, etc. Teenagers who have controlling parents may adopt some of their parents' fears and insecurities, which makes it hard for them to construct an identity apart from their parents and gain independence.

- **You struggle to react to your child calmly.** You may constantly look over your child's shoulder, expecting them to behave in ways they shouldn't. At any sudden mistake, you may be quick to reprimand your child and exaggerate your reaction. For example, you might yell at your child for staring at the TV when they are supposed to be doing their homework. The yelling is an exaggerated reaction to what is a common distraction.

If you have identified with any of these behaviors, try to recognize the opportunity presented to update your parenting approach! Now that you know that you may sometimes come across as being critical, you can learn ways to continue guiding your child's behaviors without hurting their self-esteem.

Strategies to Attack Bad Behaviors, Without Attacking Your Child

Young girls are extremely sensitive to how they are perceived by others. Perhaps this has to do with how they are conditioned from a young age to be agreeable and cooperative. Couple this with hidden ADHD symptoms, and you have a young girl who feels a sense of shame and embarrassment due to not being able to behave appropriately.

The last thing your daughter needs is more criticism, on top of what they already receive at school or amongst their peer groups. As their parent, you can address problem behaviors through constructive criticism, so that you target the behavior and not your child.

Think of constructive criticism as redirecting your child's behavior, instead of changing who they are, or making decisions on their behalf. To develop confidence and self-respect, it is important for your child to feel like they are still in control of their lives and that they have the power to choose what is good for them.

What makes criticism constructive is the fact that it provides just enough guidance to address and correct undesirable behaviors, without creating expectations or being overbearing.

Of course, this doesn't mean that your child won't face consequences whenever they behave badly. In fact, there will be occasions when it is more appropriate to move directly to issuing consequences without giving any criticism. However, the situation may be set up, the aim of constructive criticism is to educate your child on acceptable behaviors and how they can do better next time.

There are five strategies that you can practice the next time you offer constructive criticism:

Strategy 1: Take a Moment to Pause Before Giving Criticism

Take a few minutes to breathe and reflect on the purpose of the criticism. It is almost always never a good idea to give criticism when you are feeling stressed, angry, or overwhelmed. Since you want the best for your child, you want to make sure that you have given some thought to what you want to say, and how it might possibly impact them.

A few questions you can ask yourself during this time are:

- Will this criticism help my child learn the difference between acceptable and unacceptable behaviors?

- How do I want my child to walk away feeling after the discussion?

- Does this criticism align with the values I teach my child?

- Is it really necessary to give this criticism? What would happen if I didn't?

Note that criticism is not always necessary to give. For one, children will be children. There are some childish behaviors that are common in children and are due to being in a certain stage of development. If the behavior in question doesn't affect your child's or your family's well-being or safety, perhaps setting a boundary or issuing a consequence for a boundary violation is more appropriate.

Strategy 2: Focus on the "How"

Your approach to giving constructive criticism is what your child will ultimately remember, long after they have forgotten about the offense. Circling back to the discussion about how children with ADHD respond to rewards and punishment, how you give criticism can impact your child's motivation and follow through to complete tasks.

Below are some of the things to remember when planning your approach:

- Remember that your child has an ego just like you, and can be hurt by harsh or negative words. Craft your message in a way that considers their feelings. Even though they are little people, they deserve respect too.

- Target the behavior, not your child. Have an open discussion about what you saw that you didn't like, and explain why that behavior is inappropriate. Make it clear to your child that it is their behavior that upsets you, not them as a person.

- Avoid labeling your child based on their actions. Everyone makes mistakes, but we are not defined by them. For example, a child who procrastinates to complete assignments isn't a lazy person. They are simply demotivated or struggling to maintain focus.

- Don't bring up the past. Keep your message focused on what has recently occurred. Constructive criticism is future-oriented, meaning it seeks to present solutions on how a person can improve moving forward.

- Remember to give constructive criticism privately. Respect your child's dignity by correcting their behaviors away from the public. Find an appropriate time to speak with them after the event or situation has unfolded, when it is just the two of you. If you need to correct the behavior immediately, ask to speak with them on the side.

Strategy 3: Ask for Permission and Give More Control

Consider that your criticism is a critique of your child's behaviors. You are essentially sharing your opinion on how they behave, work, structure their time, communicate, etc. If somebody were to come to you and give you unsolicited criticism of your behaviors, how would you feel? Probably ambushed, defensive, or extremely frustrated.

Since you are raising your child to have a strong sense of self, it is important to show respect to them whenever possible. Asking for permission before sharing criticism is one way to respect your child's autonomy and give them a sense of choice in the matter.

Here are a few ways to ask for permission:

- Make sure that it is an appropriate time to have the discussion. You might say, "I would like to speak to you about the recent argument we had. Is this a good time for you?"

- Use "I" statements, such as "I have something on my mind that I would like to share," or "I have some information that would be helpful."

- Give them an opportunity to respond or share their own ideas after giving criticism. You might say, "Now that you have heard what I have to say, what are your thoughts?"

Approaching criticism in this way creates space for dialogue and effective problem-solving. Your child won't feel controlled or subjugated to act in certain ways; instead, they will be curious and cooperative.

Strategy 4: Make the Criticism Specific

A study looking at the performance of high school students found that unclear and general criticism is one of the most frustrating aspects of receiving feedback from teachers (Evans, 2013). In order for criticism to be constructive, it must be specific. But what does this actually mean?

Specific criticism identifies specific behaviors that need to be corrected. Instead of saying, "I don't like the way you speak to me," which could be considered vague and not useful, you might say, "I don't feel respected when you interrupt me while I am speaking." What makes the latter specific is that it identifies the incorrect behavior, and even goes as far as mentioning the negative impact.

Focus on providing enough information to help your child learn what is acceptable and unacceptable behavior. You can even use Harvard's Situation-Behavior-Impact model to structure your criticism in a way that will be helpful for your child. The model consists of three steps, namely:

- **Situation:** Describe the place and time that the behavior took place. E.g., "When we went to the supermarket early this morning."

- **Behavior:** Describe the behavior you witnessed or heard. E.g., "I saw you picking up products from the grocery aisles, even though I told you to walk next to me and only look with your eyes."

- **Impact:** Describe the thoughts, emotions, and actions the behavior triggered. E.g., "I felt upset because it showed you were not listening to my instructions."

How you describe the impact will vary depending on your child's age. For instance, there are certain emotions that younger children may not be able to understand, such as feeling hesitant, betrayed, or rejected. Therefore, adjust your language accordingly, so that your child is able to reflect on their behaviors and begin to see why certain actions are not tolerated.

Strategy 5: Be a Good Role Model

Children learn more by watching your behaviors as a parent than what you preach. Before offering constructive criticism, assess how well you live up to the values and expectations you instill in your child. For instance, if you don't like how your daughter speaks to you, reflect on how you communicate with other family members, like your spouse or older children, or even friends and colleagues. Are you patient? Do you allow them to speak without interrupting? Do you often raise your voice?

You can also help your child learn how to respond well to criticism by playing games where they need to rate your skills or final outcomes. For example, you might start a cooking competition with another family member and ask your child to taste both meals and rate which one they prefer.

When rating the meals, get them to practice some of the strategies we have discussed in this section, like being mindful of your feelings, focusing on the "how," and making the criticism specific. Afterward, discuss how receiving their feedback made you feel. Acknowledge that although it was difficult to hear that your meal wasn't perfect, they made really good points that you can use to improve your skills.

How to Use Positive Reinforcement to Improve Behavior

Constructive criticism is one way of correcting your child's troublesome behaviors without dampening their spirits. Another way, which we touched on earlier, is using positive reinforcement.

When you catch a child misbehaving, the last thing on your mind is to find a strength that you can praise them for. What you may be focused on is showing your child that what they are doing is wrong. However, as we have seen, children with ADHD are more sensitive to punishment than non-ADHD children. This means that instead of pointing out the negatives, you can encourage changed behaviors by highlighting the positives.

For example, your little girl has reached the stage where they are able to help out around the house. But they don't seem too excited about the idea of being assigned chores. For them, chores feel like a form of punishment. After all, why would they want to steal time away from watching TV or playing outside?

Seeing how anti-chores your child is, you would need to increase the incentives of completing chores. In other words, your aim would be to make the idea so attractive that they willingly perform the task without needing to beg them. If you decide to go the positive reinforcement route, you might praise your child for contributing to the well-being of the family by doing the chore. While they are still contemplating the chore and deciding how they feel about it, you can mention how thankful you are that they are contributing to the well-being of the family and just how important this task is.

Focusing on the sense of achievement that your child can feel during and after completing the chore can motivate them to get it done. You may even assign them a big and bright star next to their name on the roster, whenever they have successfully completed the chore.

Offering positive reinforcement doesn't always need to be something elaborate, or linked to bad behavior. Sometimes, it could be as simple as cheering, giving a high five, saying "I'm proud of you," or giving a warm cuddle. All of these behaviors communicate love and acceptance of your child. What is more important is deciding on what kinds of behaviors you would like to positively reinforce. For example, do you want to positively reinforce completing a homework assignment, or putting in the effort to sit on a chair for 20 minutes, trying your best to not get distracted? What you reinforce is completely up to you, although there are a few positive behaviors to consider:

- showing commitment

- sharing toys

- saying "please" and "thank you"

- being a good friend

- completing a chore

- remembering to pack the school bag

- compromising and being flexible

- volunteering to assist other family members

- being patient

- sharing their thoughts and feelings

There are also a few tips to remember when giving positive reinforcement, which includes:

- **Get the timing right.** The right time to use positive reinforcement is when your child is learning a new skill or practicing a healthy habit. You will need to be vigilant and catch them during the act so that your praise is genuine and realistic.

- **Tie rewards with good behaviors.** If you are planning on giving your child tangible rewards, make sure that they are linked with good behavior, rather than being random. Not only can this create a positive association in your child's brain, but it also motivates them to repeat the good behavior in the future.

- **Don't give attention to bad behavior.** Attention is a form of positive reinforcement. When your child sees that they are getting a reaction from you every time they act poorly, they have enough of an incentive to continue misbehaving. Learn to ignore attention-seeking behavior, like whining, tantrums, cursing, or mocking laughter. Simply follow through with issuing a consequence for their actions, and later on discussing what you didn't like about their behavior.

When used appropriately, positive reinforcement can be an effective tool to manage troublesome behaviors and inspire positive and healthy ones. In most cases, emphasizing the good that you see in your child can empower them to create standards for themselves and keep their bad habits at bay.

Chapter Takeaways

- Due to their disruptive behaviors, adults tend to correct children with ADHD more than neurotypical children. This means that a girl child with ADHD is more likely to hear "No!" several times a day.

- Girls with ADHD are more sensitive to failure, criticism, and punishment. To avoid being criticized, they might avoid taking on challenges that feel punishing or place excessive pressure on themselves to act appropriately.

- Children of parents who are overly critical tend to experience ongoing and persistent ADHD symptoms that continue into adolescence.

- Instead of being too harsh or negative, parents can learn to correct their children's behaviors by providing constructive criticism, which can include being mindful of the child's feelings, attacking the behavior not the child, and being a good role model.

- Positive reinforcement is another effective tool that can be used to incentivize good behaviors and steer the child in a positive direction.

Chapter 4:

Don't Get Lost in the

Daydream

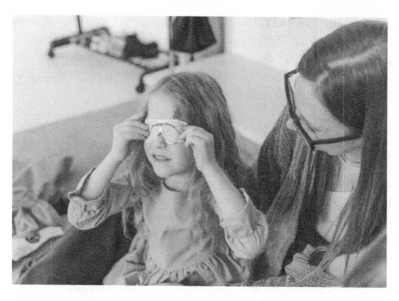

They who dream by day are cognizant of many things which escape those who dream only by night. –Edgar Allen Poe

Inattentive ADHD vs. Maladaptive Daydreaming

One of the hallmark symptoms of inattentive ADHD is constant daydreaming. Young girls and even teenagers may frequently drift away and get lost in their thoughts. This not only happens when they are left to work on a task; it can also happen in the middle of conversations.

Since inattentive ADHD is hardly recognized in girls, doctors can misdiagnose the symptoms as being signs of maladaptive daydreaming. While both conditions are rooted in inattentiveness, they present themselves differently, and therefore cannot be treated the same.

Children who experience maladaptive daydreaming intentionally have all-consuming daydreams that interfere with their daily functioning. Inattentive ADHD, on the other hand, causes children to get easily distracted by thoughts or stimuli in their environment. For example, a child with inattentive ADHD can daydream, but this is often due to mind wandering, not purposeful daydreaming.

The big difference between the two conditions is choice. Maladaptive daydreaming is choosing to get lost in a fantasy world that feels much more pleasurable than reality, whereas, with inattentive ADHD, daydreaming is the outcome of not being able to pay attention to the present moment.

It is important for parents to understand the differences between these two conditions because they can affect treatment. For instance, a young girl with inattentive ADHD who frequently daydreams may simply take stimulant medications to manage mind wandering. If they are misdiagnosed with maladaptive daydreaming, the doctor may recommend psychotherapy to address the addiction to daydreaming. In the long run, this won't improve their short attention span, distractibility, and other symptoms of inattentive ADHD.

This can also work the other way. If a young girl with maladaptive daydreaming is misdiagnosed with inattentive ADHD, the doctor may prescribe stimulant medications, which will only "increase focus" on their fantasies and worsen their condition.

Why Daydreaming Isn't as Bad as You Think

Daydreaming is putting your attention elsewhere. You could be in the office, but thinking about what you are going to make for dinner. Or fixing dinner and thinking about your long to-do list and whether you have checked off everything. The fact is adults daydream just as easily and frequently as children; however, when we do it, we aren't told to snap out of it!

As a parent of a child with ADHD, particularly inattentive ADHD, you may fear that your child's daydreaming habit may cause serious problems, like performing poorly at school or being perceived by teachers as troublesome. However, if you consider that daydreaming is simply getting distracted by mostly pleasant thoughts, you can discover how it can be something positive in your child's life.

Below are just a few ways that daydreaming can be something good for your child:

- **Daydreaming can be a form of stress relief.** When your child is feeling restless in class, or overwhelmed by the number of stimuli in their environment, drifting away in their thoughts can offer a temporary escape that helps them self-regulate and return feeling rejuvenated.

- **Daydreaming can promote creative thinking.** Being lost in thought can be productive, especially when your child is figuring out ways to solve a problem or visualizing how they might carry themselves in future outcomes. This type of creative thinking can be a preventative measure to manage stress and anxiety related to future scenarios.

- **Daydreaming can support goal-setting.** When you and your child have agreed to work on a few goals together, daydreaming can help them visualize achieving those positive results. This can be a great way to incentivize investing physical and mental effort into improving skills and learning new habits.

- **Daydreaming causes your child to be more open-minded.** When your child daydreams, they transcend the world of physical limitations and enter into the world of possibilities. This can broaden their thinking, increase self-awareness, and help them develop a tolerance for other people.

- **Daydreaming prepares your child for the future.** The best inventors, entrepreneurs, and thought leaders throughout the ages nurtured their imaginations from a very young age. Some of the best ideas that we rely on for everyday functioning, like cars, mobile phones, and online services, started out as fantasies and imagery in someone's mind.

The traditional school system might frown upon daydreaming, but perhaps they are only looking at it from one angle. Sure, daydreaming can be considered a type of procrastination. But it certainly doesn't harm your child the same way procrastinating does. When controlled, it can enrich your child's life and be used as a healthy coping mechanism.

Heck, daydreaming can also be beneficial for you! Consider the following exercises that inspire you to get lost in your thoughts:

- Do you have a favorite daydream that you frequently think about when you are feeling bored, demotivated, or happy? Take five minutes to travel to that place in your mind and enjoy the fantasy.

- Think about a goal that you hope to achieve in the near future. Make sure it is a personal goal that involves improving certain aspects of your life. Visualize the goal unfolding over several months or years. Notice where you are, who is with you, what you are doing, and how you feel.

- Has there been a personal crisis plaguing your mind recently? Take five minutes to think about the crisis, but this time try to look at it from a different perspective. See whether you can come up with an unconventional solution to solve the crisis, or at least improve it.

How did you feel practicing these exercises? Based on what you have just experienced, would daydreaming be something you encourage in your child?

How to Help Your Child Monitor Their Daydreaming

Daydreaming is not a danger or weakness. The only time it may start to become a problem is when it interferes with your child's daily functioning, such as in the case of maladaptive daydreaming. But with the right interventions and guidance, you can help your child regulate daydreaming.

If you are concerned about your child's daydreaming and want to step in, here are a few useful suggestions:

- **Avoid speaking negatively about your child's daydreaming or forcing them to stop.** Remember positive reinforcement? Your child is more likely to succeed at regulating their daydreaming when they are taught how to be self-aware and praised whenever they refocus their attention on a present task.

- **Teach your child self-monitoring skills.** Use tools like journals, charts, or worksheets to help your child record each time they daydream, and for how long their mind wanders. Due to the sophistication of this skill, it may be more suitable for older kids (more on self-monitoring in the section below).

- **Teach your child grounding techniques.** To ground yourself is to activate your five senses and fully focus on what is happening right now. There are a range of grounding techniques that you can teach your child to help them refocus their attention, like running their hands under cold or hot water, sucking on ice, doing 10 jumping jacks, and singing along to their favorite tune.

- **Improve your child's nutrition.** Reassess the kinds of foods your child eats and look for ways to incorporate more brain foods, such as leafy green vegetables, fatty fish like salmon or tuna, berries, walnuts, and low-fat dairy products.

- **Make sure your child is getting adequate sleep.** One of the symptoms associated with ADHD is insomnia. Not getting enough quality sleep can lead to low energy and daydreaming during the day. If your child isn't already on a bedtime schedule, consider putting them on one. Stick to the same sleep and wake times for several weeks, until their natural body clock adjusts.

The aim of these strategies is to create enough opportunity for your child to daydream, but at the same time, teach them how to monitor their own behavior so that it doesn't become a threat to their well-being.

Self-Monitoring Strategies for Girls

Executive functioning skills are mental processes children learn that help them pay attention, follow instructions, plan ahead, and manage multiple tasks. Children with ADHD usually lack these skills, which makes it difficult for them to stay organized, recall information, or focus and follow through on tasks.

One of the steps parents can take to reinforce executive functioning skills is to teach their children self-monitoring strategies. These are simple exercises and activities to increase their awareness of what is happening inside and around them. A typical example of self-monitoring is recognizing feeling upset, identifying the specific situation that triggered the emotion, and taking a few deep breaths to calm down.

There are three steps that must be followed to practice self-monitoring:

Observation

The first step is to pay attention to the thought, emotion, or action that is appearing in the moment. A simple way to teach kids how to observe stimuli is to ask them sensory-based questions:

- What can you hear with your ears?

- What can you smell with your nose?

- What can you see with your eyes?

- What can you taste inside your mouth?

- What thoughts are you having inside your head?

- What can you touch with your hands?

- What can you feel inside your heart?

A young girl who frequently blurts out information in class might hear themselves speaking while the teacher is presenting the lesson, and see the disapproving look on their teacher's face. The parent can step in and ask the child what conclusion they might draw from these actions taking place simultaneously. The conclusion might be: When I talk while the teacher is presenting the lesson, it makes her or him upset.

Observing thoughts and actions may be easier than drawing patterns or conclusions from them. Your child may need a great deal of practice and reflection before they can make connections between the various stimuli they observe. Continue to ask them what their observations mean, and what clues or evidence they have to prove them.

Recording

The second step of self-monitoring is where children take action based on what they observed. They are able to identify inappropriate behavior and find ways of correcting them. There are various tools used to record and keep track of behaviors, such as:

- journaling

- creating checklists

- daily behavior assessments

- noting each time an undesirable behavior is acted out (i.e., Each time the child interrupts the teacher)

- creating targets, and measuring how close they came to reaching them.

Parents can assist young children with recording and monitoring behaviors; however, older children are encouraged to practice this step on their own. This will give them a sense of autonomy and keep them accountable for positively adjusting their behaviors.

Introspection

The final step of self-monitoring is practicing introspection, which is the process of examining your thoughts and emotions. Many times, children with ADHD are aware of their disruptive behaviors or poor choices but feel helpless breaking the habit. They can use introspection to go behind the behavior and target the thoughts or emotions that bring up the urges or desires.

For example, a teenage girl might realize that they only daydream during classes they don't enjoy, like math or science, and find it much easier to concentrate during classes that excite them, like drama or geography. This level of awareness can be useful to monitor and slowly break the habit of daydreaming during those undesirable classes. Every time they catch themselves zoning out, they may recognize what is taking place (and why it is happening) and then voluntarily refocus their attention on the work at hand.

Introspection is another skill that would be more appropriate to teach older kids who are able to travel deeper in their minds and make the connection between thoughts, emotions, and behaviors.

Mindfulness Practice Made Easy

Mindfulness is an Eastern practice that has made its way to the West, over the past two decades. The idea behind it is to train the mind to pay attention to what is happening at every moment. While a little mind wandering isn't bad for your child, there are times when it can contribute to increased stress and anxiety, particularly when they focus on unpleasant thoughts and feelings.

Research has shown that regular practice of mindfulness, whether it is through meditation, intentional breathing, or mindfully performing tasks, can improve mental well-being, assist in regulating emotions, and improve attention. It has also been recommended by doctors as a psychotherapy treatment option for conditions like ADHD, intermittent explosive disorder (IED), and obsessive compulsive disorder (OCD).

The best way to teach your child mindfulness is to incorporate the practice into their daily routine. Find different situations where you can teach your child how to take a pause, observe, and appreciate what is happening in the moment. Below are a few useful suggestions:

- **Throughout the day, practice taking "brain breaks."** Brain breaks are deliberate five-minute pauses where your child leaves whatever they are busy with and takes deep breaths. The aim is for them to not think about anything, but just focus on feeling calm.

- **Take listening walks.** Go on a relaxing walk with your child and ask them to focus on the different sounds they can hear. Challenge them to notice as many sounds as possible, or have a discussion about what happy moment each sound reminds them of.

- **Mindfully eat a snack.** When snack time approaches, sit down with your child and mindfully engage with the food. Encourage them to chew slower, take breaks to breathe during each bite, and notice the different flavors in the food. You can also choose to eat in silence and allow your child to fully engage with your food. Afterward, you can have a discussion about their sensory experience.

- **Download a mindfulness app.** There are a variety of mindfulness apps available on the market that can assist children of different age groups to calm their minds and regulate their emotions. One such app that is appropriate for children aged 5–10 years old is the "Stop, Think & Breathe" app. It contains a range of mindfulness activities that can help your child focus, feel relaxed, and sleep better at night.

- **Create a mindfulness family ritual.** Think about a mindfulness activity that the whole family can practice on a regular basis. For instance, you might enforce a "quiet time" between 4:00–5:00 p.m. where the entire family unplugs from technology and spends their time on calming activities, like taking a nap or reading.

In this fast-paced world, living a mindful lifestyle can significantly improve your family's well-being. Continue to look for different mindful habits that you can introduce to your family to promote living in the moment and facing each day as it comes.

Chapter Takeaways

- Common signs of inattentiveness in girls include getting easily distracted, daydreaming, or gazing out of the window. These signs can often be confused as symptoms of maladaptive daydreaming, but that is a separate and different condition.

- The difference between inattentive ADHD and maladaptive daydreaming is that the former causes difficulty paying attention, while the latter is a deliberate choice to get lost in a daydream, to the extent of being unproductive.

- Daydreaming is not a destructive behavior per se, since it can enhance creativity, promote future planning, improve resiliency, and cause children to be more open-minded. Nonetheless, parents can teach their children various strategies, like self-monitoring or mindfulness, to monitor and manage their own behavior.

Chapter 5:

The Clock Is Ticking...

If you want to make good use of your time, you've got to know what's most important and then give it all you've got. –Lee Iacocca

Can Girls With ADHD Learn Time Management?

The topic of time management is one that is often brought up when discussing symptoms of ADHD. However, what we shouldn't forget is that poor time management is a skill that we can all learn or improve. Sure, children and adults with ADHD may need more reinforcement to manage their time wisely, but it isn't an issue that is exclusive to them. Therefore, as you go through this chapter, reflect on ways that you manage your time, and assess whether some of the strategies provided would be beneficial for you too!

Since ADHD is a neurodevelopmental disorder, it affects memory and the ability to plan ahead and organize tasks. This means that children with ADHD tend to find it much harder to grasp the concept of punctuality or following routines. Some of the ways that poor time management can show up in their day-to-day lives include:

1. Time blindness

A child with ADHD (both hyperactive and inattentive type) is often unaware of how long tasks take to accomplish. It is as though they are working on their own schedule, blind to the allocated time frames or deadlines of tasks. For girls with ADHD in particular, their perfectionist tendencies might cause them to redo the same task, over and over again, until it meets their standards. The upside is that they can produce exceptional work, but the downside is they may struggle to complete it on time.

2. Difficulty planning ahead

Your child may also find it hard to grasp the idea of future events, such as a class assignment due in two weeks. They may feel confused about why they were told about the assignment today if it is only required in two weeks. What may seem to parents to be signs of procrastination (and may very well be), like putting off studying for an upcoming test, may sometimes be the inability to budget time and plan ahead.

3. Distractibility

Another symptom of poor time management is being easily distracted. This can be a recurring experience for children with inattentive ADHD. It takes a minor sound, movement, thought, or interesting object to shift their focus away from what they are busy with, and onto something else. Being distracted easily stretches the length of time to complete tasks, which makes following a schedule that much harder.

These three factors don't excuse your child's poor time management skills, but they can help to explain why something that may come easier for you, or your other non-ADHD children, takes more effort to teach to your child. The good news is that your child can learn how to manage their time wisely—and you might be the best person to guide them!

Time Management Strategies for Young Girls and Teens

Time management skills become more valuable the older your child gets. For instance, a teacher might not show concern when a preschooler struggles to finish their homework assignment or hands it in late. But they will certainly be unforgiving when a pre-teen or teenager displays the same behavior.

The same allowances could be reflected at home. You may not be too concerned about your preschooler leaving their room untidy or taking hours to complete their homework. But when your pre-teen or teenager can't tidy up after themselves or manage their time properly, you may feel frustrated.

It is therefore important to start teaching your daughter effective time management strategies, from a young age. The fewer excuses you make for them, the more independent and reliable they will be as they reach their teen years. Remind yourself that you're not only training your child to pick up their own load at home; you are also preparing them to pick up their load at school.

Below are age-appropriate time management strategies that you can teach your child:

Girls Aged 3–8

Children who are very young don't know much about time management. Plus, since they haven't learned many of the executive functioning skills, it is up to parents to expose their children to basic time management strategies.

A great way to do this is to get your child on a routine. This could be a morning routine, bedtime routine, mealtime routine, or playtime routine. Through establishing routines, you can teach them about sequences (i.e., first step, second step, and third step). For example, a morning routine may include three steps:

- First step: Brush your teeth.

- Second step: Take a bath.

- Third step: Eat cereal.

As your child gets accustomed to a basic routine, you can teach them how to follow a full day's routine, which may include a combination of smaller routines. For example, in a day, they may follow a morning, school, homework, playtime, and bedtime routine. This may sound like a lot for your child. However, if you take time to practice each individual routine— and keep the sequence short and basic—combining multiple routines may not be too disorientating.

Note that following a routine is only the basics of time management. It teaches your child how to follow through with tasks and keep up with their daily schedule, but you and other caregivers involved will need to still monitor how long they spend on each task or make sure they are not distracted during tasks.

Girls Aged 9–12

The pre-teen stage is when you can start to introduce and reinforce the concept of time. Your task during these years is to help your child understand how to tell the time, determine the sequence of past, present, and future events, as well as create their own routines.

Your child will learn about time around third grade, but you can carry out activities at home to practice what they have been taught at school. Now is probably a good time to buy a clock for your house—preferably an analog clock—so that they understand that time moves, and learn how to pace and organize themselves in relation to the ticking clock.

Practice placing daily tasks or events in context by telling the time with your child. For instance, you can ask them what time you should wake them up in the morning—6:00 a.m. or 6:30 a.m.? Based on their answer, both of you can assess whether that is enough time to prepare for school. You might say, "If you wake up at 6:30 a.m., how much time will that give you to prepare for school?" Or before completing a task, ask your child how much time they will need (i.e., 30 minutes), and what time that will be on the clock (i.e., 1:30 p.m.)

When teaching your child about time, it might also help to buy them a timer. This can be really useful for a child who suffers from time blindness. Before they complete an activity, ask your child how much time they will need (it might help to give them three options to choose from).

Set the timer and give them space to complete the task. When the timer goes off, check back with them and see how much progress they have made. You can ask, "Do you feel that was enough time to complete this task? How much more time do you need?" A child who doesn't understand the concept of time might initially allocate five minutes for a task that takes an average kid 30 minutes to complete. Try not to correct them by allocating the right amount of time. Let them figure out on their own how to budget time for each task.

Girls Aged 13–17

Time management becomes a necessity for older children. Without it, they will struggle to keep up with the demands of their lifestyles. Plus, the involvement of parents starts to decrease the older children get, so it is important to prepare them to manage their busy lifestyles independently.

What does time management look like for a teenager? Creating plans and staying organized!

There are many useful tools that you can introduce to your child to help them keep up with the demands of home and school. The first is encouraging them to use calendars and planners. Calendars and planners are great for a teenage girl with ADHD because they help her make sense of different pieces of information, and how much time they will need to allocate for each task.

Time blocking is a technique that works well on calendars and planners (both digital and physical). It involves "blocking out" time slots to complete various tasks to avoid overlaps or over-committing. Each day, your child is able to see how their schedule looks, when they will have free time, and if there is any more space to add more tasks. This can also manage your child's anxiety by helping her anticipate busy days and mentally prepare themselves.

Another useful tool is creating to-do lists or checklists. This quick and simple activity works the same way as sequencing. On a piece of paper, your child can write down immediate tasks that they need to complete within a space of time. Both writing tasks down and checking off tasks on the list offer an incentive for the brain to continue working diligently. I'm sure you can admit—there is a sense of accomplishment you feel whenever you look at a completed to-do list at the end of the day!

Having to-do lists or checklists can also encourage your child to identify priority tasks. The truth is they won't always have enough time during the day to complete everything they scheduled on their calendar or planner. Therefore, it can be useful to start the day by identifying urgent or really important tasks and writing them down in a list. These will be the tasks that take priority and must ideally be completed first. Examples of priority tasks include studying for an upcoming test, completing chores, and remembering to take ADHD medication.

Solutions for Staying Organized

Besides the common symptoms of ADHD, another reason why your child may have poor time management is that they are disorganized. When your space is in shambles, it is difficult to think straight or keep up with daily tasks.

Disorganization may feature in various ways in your child's life. Perhaps they are the type of child to forget important school materials at home and only remember when it is time to use them. Or maybe they have a hard time keeping their workspace or bedroom clutter-free. Of course, with children, sloppiness is common, and it would be unfair for us to expect perfection. However, a little bit of organizational skills can go a long way to improving their mental well-being and helping them take pride in their routines.

Children who are on ADHD medication can show improvements in executive functions like staying organized. But they will still need to be monitored and given positive reinforcement to maintain good organizational habits. Below are some of the ways you can help your child stay organized:

- **Provide your child with all of the materials they will need to complete a task.** To help your child overcome the inner resistance to complete a task, make sure they are given every supply necessary to get started. For example, if they are completing math homework, place their math book, pen, ruler, highlighter, and calculator on their desk to increase follow-through.

- **Color code books by subject.** Children with ADHD can be forgetful and easily misplace things. Color code their books by subject, to make them easier to trace at school and around the house. At the end of each day, you can also ask your child to check that all red, yellow, and orange books are sitting in the right piles and trays.

- **Create more storage space.** All of your child's belongings should have a "home," If you don't have space in your cupboards, purchase large bins and assign labels for each. Keep their toys separate from their school books, clothes, and any other loose items. Make it your child's responsibility to tidy up after themselves and store away their belongings in the correct bins.

- **Don't forget to offer plenty of positive reinforcement.** Be mindful of how much brain power it takes for your child to stay organized. Whenever they follow through with a clean-up task, be generous with your praise. If you would like them to develop a habit of staying organized, consider creating a rewards system where they can earn points every time they practice organizational skills.

- **Post reminders around the house.** Help your child remember important information, like which days to complete chores, or when assignments are due, by posting reminders around the house. Be creative in how you visually display information. For instance, the family house rules might be on a large laminated poster, the weekly chores might be written on a chalkboard, and upcoming school events or assignment deadlines might be posted on a pin board.

What's important to note about the strategies above is that you aren't doing the work for your child. You are simply making the work a lot easier by creating more incentives for your child to do it.

Build Your Child's Routines

If your child is still too young to create their own routine, you can also help them stay organized by providing simple routines they can follow. To make routines effective, they must be child-friendly, realistic, and easy to memorize. When setting up routines, consider whether your child will be able to perform the task on a consistent basis without feeling overwhelmed. The tasks you add should be second-nature to your child; things they already do without much effort.

Here are a few routines that you can adopt to help your child stay organized during the day:

Morning Routine

- Turn off the morning alarm.

- Brush teeth, wash face, and comb hair.

- Change clothes (wear clothes that were picked out last night).

- Eat breakfast at the kitchen table.

- Check to see if all books and assignments are inside the school bag.

- Wait by the car at a certain time.

Homework Routine

- Eat the prepared lunch after arriving from school.

- Spend 30 minutes playing or doing something creative.

- Grab the necessary books and supplies and head to the workstation. Don't bring the entire school bag or any other materials that aren't related to the work at hand.

- Spend 10 minutes reading through homework instructions and asking questions.

- Set a timer for the first round of completing homework. Decide on a reasonable amount of time to sit at the desk without getting up (e.g., 5–10 minute intervals).

- When the timer goes off, get up, stretch your legs, and go to the restroom.

- Pack books and supplies inside your school bag after the homework is complete.

Dinner Routine

- Assist mom or dad with dinner, by either helping to prepare the meal, keeping the kitchen counter clean, or setting the dinner table (or any other age-appropriate task).

- Sit down at the dinner table at a certain time. Make sure that cell phones are put away.

- Have casual conversations and share a little more about your day.

- Assist mom or dad to clean up the kitchen afterward (or any other age-appropriate task).

Bedtime Routine

- Put away toys and turn off the TV.

- Enjoy a healthy snack at the kitchen table.

- Lay out clothes for tomorrow.

- Take a bath, brush teeth, and wear pajamas.

- Read a book with mom or dad.

- Enjoy bedtime cuddles then go to sleep.

How to Check-In With Your Child's Progress

Ideally, you would like your child to have great time management and organizational skills so that they can be left alone to complete tasks. However, since children with ADHD cannot naturally maintain focus for very long, you will need to check in with them and see if they are doing what they are supposed to.

Here are a few questions you can ask when checking in with your child:

- What are you looking forward to today?

- What is on your mind?

- Are you comfortable working here?

- How can I support you?

- What aspect of the task are you struggling with?

- How is your schedule looking for today?

- Will you need my assistance with anything?

- Do you need a short break?

- Are you hungry?

- Have you had a nap today?

Note that check-ins don't need to be based on the tasks they are working on. You could ask questions about their physical, mental, and emotional well-being too. For example, instead of asking your child how the task is going, you can ask how comfortable they are sitting on the chair, or see if they need a glass of water. Taking care of your child's holistic well-being is what will enhance their focus.

Chapter Takeaways

- Time management and staying organized are executive function skills. They require a good memory, careful planning, and the ability to follow through with tasks.

- Children with ADHD, particularly the inattentive type, struggle with these skills and may need extra support and positive reinforcement to learn them.

- While younger children aren't expected to be punctual and organized, older kids may experience a lot of backlash when they aren't able to plan, meet deadlines, or clean up after themselves.

- At every age, there are effective strategies you can teach your child to prepare them for life in the real world. These include helping them learn and follow routines, tell time, and use planning tools to stay organized.

Chapter 6:

Mirror, Mirror, On the Wall

Believe in yourself and all that you are. Know that there is something inside you that is greater than any obstacle. –Swami Vivekananda

Girls With ADHD and Self-Esteem Issues

Fluctuating moods are common in children with ADHD. One minute your child may feel happy and social, the next they may feel overwhelmed by their ADHD symptoms. It is also not uncommon for them to experience cognitive distortions, which are faulty or irrational thoughts that don't match reality. These cognitive distortions can become so grievous that they cause your child to doubt themselves or have the wrong assumption about what is happening around them.

As a parent, your initial reaction is to show compassion because you understand the pressure your child may be feeling. However, they may not always be so kind toward themselves. Girls with ADHD are more likely to get frustrated with themselves every time they don't "act right." This may be in part due to the cultural standards that are imposed on girls to be polite, docile, and emotionally regulated.

Whenever they fail to meet an expectation at school, in public, or at home, they might punish themselves by entertaining harmful thoughts, like thinking they are not good enough or something is inherently wrong with them. What's also interesting to note about girls with ADHD is that they are more likely to internalize their stress and anger than express it outwardly. Once again, this has to do with the shame of being a "bad girl" or displaying any signs of aggression. This is particularly why girls with ADHD tend to be diagnosed with comorbid conditions like anxiety and depression.

What does all of this have to do with self-esteem issues?

The combination of having "invisible" symptoms that are often disguised and left undiagnosed, as well as feeling the societal pressure to behave like a traditional girl, causes young girls with ADHD to experience identity issues. They may struggle to accept themselves for who they are and learn to embrace their differences. In most cases, having a low self-esteem opens the door to self-harming behaviors, like experimenting with drugs and alcohol, perfectionism, or developing an eating disorder.

As a loving and supportive parent, you can assist your child in forming a stable sense of self and learning how to feel comfortable in their own skin. Like any other intervention, helping your child cultivate a healthy self-esteem should start from a young age, and continue during their teen years. However, there is no such thing as being "too late" to help improve your child's self-esteem, and if you haven't yet begun, now is a good time!

How to Help Your Daughter Discover Her Girl Power

There is nothing more demotivating for your child than constantly being reminded that they can't perform tasks that other children can perform effortlessly. They dread that moment in class when a teacher asks for their homework submission but only remember then that they even had an assignment due. Or that moment in a social setting when they are the last person to pick up on how uncomfortable everyone feels around them.

There are numerous times when your child's sense of self-worth will be tested. If it isn't at home, then it will certainly come from the outside world. Unfortunately, society still stigmatizes children and adults with ADHD, choosing to see them as "lazy," "socially awkward," or "absent-minded." But there are also plenty of strategies that you can teach your child to prepare them for the unforgiving world and activate their inner girl power. Below are three that you can work on together.

Strategy 1: Challenge Negative Thinking

Negative thoughts are usually fueled with emotion and passion, making them seem valid and rational. Since they come with so much emotion and passion, your child may find it difficult to challenge or change them. However, by getting to know what negative thoughts sound like, they can get better at catching cognitive distortions and dealing effectively with those unwanted thoughts.

Below are examples of five common cognitive distortions, with examples:

1. **Mental filtering**

Mental filtering is the process of looking at only the negatives of a situation and ignoring the positives. What you end up with is an event that seems as though it only had negative outcomes, without any kind of positive experience.

For example, your child might receive their test marks and feel disappointed at getting a 60% average (as opposed to their target of 75%), even though this is a drastic improvement from their previous test marks. The positive outcome that is ignored is the fact that they have made progress, despite not being the exact amount they were anticipating.

2. All-or-nothing thinking

All-or-nothing thinking is having an extreme view of yourself or the world. Situations are usually understood through polar opposites, like being either good or bad, fat or skinny, ugly or beautiful, smart or dumb. There is no balance or middle ground in how situations are interpreted, and this often leads to unfair assumptions.

For example, your child might be convinced they are ugly due to not receiving the attention they would like from the opposite sex. They create an association between the lack of attention and their physical appearance, which isn't a fair or rational thought process.

3. Overgeneralization

Overgeneralization occurs when past negative events or patterns are used to justify what is happening right now. Perhaps your child experienced a hurtful situation that made them feel scared, angry, or embarrassed. Whenever a similar, but unrelated, situation occurs in the present, they make a generalization and assume the past negative pattern is repeating itself.

For example, when your child gets in trouble at school for inappropriate behavior, they might think "I always get in trouble" or "Other kids never get in trouble. It's always me." What makes this overgeneralization is the use of words like "always," and "never," which make it seem as though this isolated incident is something that frequently repeats itself. This can make it difficult for them to recognize and take accountability for their wrongdoings since they feel hopeless about changing the pattern.

4. Jumping to conclusions

This is one that you may already be familiar with. Jumping to conclusions happens when your child assumes an outcome (in most cases a negative outcome) without enough information to validate their assumptions.

For example, when approaching a group of teenagers, your child might assume the group won't take kindly to them. This assumption may very well be due to overgeneralization, after experiencing a similar situation in the past; however, it is also jumping to conclusions because there isn't enough evidence about the character and attitudes of the group of teenagers to prove this assumption.

5. Emotional reasoning

Emotional reasoning is the process of judging a situation based on the emotional impact it has made. Situations that trigger undesirable emotions are perceived as being a threat, suspicious, painful, or unfair, even though in reality this may not be the case. The danger of making assumptions based on emotions is that often emotions are unreliable. Yes, they are real and powerful, but they don't reveal the full picture of what is happening. Emotions only show you what you want to see, not everything there is to see.

For example, your child may confess to not liking school. When you investigate further, you may realize that it isn't necessarily that they don't like school, but that they often feel overwhelmed by the demands of school. Another example is your child thinking that everyone hates them. When you investigate further, you may realize that it isn't that everyone hates them (that would be an overgeneralization), but that they are unable to read social cues, which makes communication with other students feel unnatural.

Identifying cognitive distortions can sometimes be tricky because they can feel like the truth, especially when there isn't any other obvious explanation for an event or situation. A great way to teach your child how to catch and challenge negative thoughts is getting them to answer unbiased questions about their thoughts, such as:

- **What thinking errors could I be making?** *Am I looking at the situation in black and white? Have I judged the situation based on how I feel? Could I be overgeneralizing?*

- **What is the effect of thinking this way?** *What are the pros and cons of maintaining this outlook? Will this thought benefit me in the future? Have I only considered my point of view? Am I emphasizing my weaknesses and downplaying my strengths?*

- **What is the evidence for this thought?** *Are there any facts to support my thought? If I told someone else this thought, would they agree with me? Could I have mistakenly chosen to see only the negatives, or jumped to conclusions? Could I be blaming myself for something that isn't my fault?*

It is much easier for your child to reframe negative thoughts and achieve more balanced thinking once they have proof that their negative thoughts are false. Instead of trying to convince your child that their negative thoughts are false, allow them to go through this process of identifying cognitive distortions and asking questions to see whether their thinking is rational or irrational.

Bear in mind, younger children, who haven't yet learned how to reflect on their own thoughts and feelings may struggle to challenge their negative thoughts. You can assist them by sitting together and going through the questions above. Show curiosity in their mental processing and raise alternative perspectives that they may not be able to see.

Strategy 2: Focus On Strengths

It takes a great deal of self-awareness, curiosity, and openness to identify positive qualities and attributes about yourself. These are skills that even adults tend to struggle with, let alone children. It is human nature to inflate what we don't like about ourselves and undermine what we love and are good at.

Girls with ADHD have a tendency of inflating their weaknesses related to their symptoms and undermining qualities that make them awesome human beings. Without parental guidance, they can easily lose touch with the positive aspects of who they are.

An important message to continuously reinforce to children with ADHD is that their condition is not a life sentence. There are no unique limitations imposed on them or opportunities they cannot obtain. Helping your child focus on their strengths is a great way to show them that living with ADHD isn't all that bad. In fact, it may even cause them to excel in certain areas of their life!

The first step is to explain to them that everyone is born with strengths, regardless of their gender, race, religion, culture, or disabilities. This means that girls have strengths just as much as boys, Hispanic people have strengths just as much as Asian people, and children with ADHD have strengths just as much as those without ADHD.

One way to prove this to your child and make it more real is to complete the strengths exercise. Grabe two separate pieces of paper and pens for you and your child. Working independently, write down a list of your child's strengths. They will come up with their own list and you will come up with one too. Use the table of strengths below for inspiration on what their strengths might be.

Honest	Caring	Trustworthy
Empathetic	Loyal	Friendly
Hard working	Generous	Kind
Resilient	Creative	Smart
Brave	Adventurous	Playful
Forgiving	Open-minded	Patient
Athletic	Sociable	Optimistic
Non-judgmental	Good problem-solver	Good sense of humor

When you have both completed your lists, share what strengths you wrote down. There will most likely be strengths that you identify in your child that they may not have identified in themselves. Explain why you believe they possess the strength by giving evidence of past situations where they displayed it. For example, "I see your bravery come out whenever we go to a doctor's visit, and you handle yourself like a true champion!"

If your child struggles with motivation and requires a little bit more support on a daily basis, you can take the opportunity to verbalize any strengths they may exhibit in the moment.

For example, if your primary schooler dreads homework time, but is able to sit at their desk for 20 minutes, you can tell them "I am so proud of you for showing patience by sitting at your desk." Or on the random occasion when your teenage daughter steps outside of their comfort zone and strikes up a conversation with someone new, you can say "I know that wasn't easy for you. I admire your openness to new experiences."

It is also important to recognize their strengths when they are showing difficulty but are still trying. For example, a child who struggles academically, but still attends extra classes and does their best to keep up with the pace of school, deserves to be told how determined, resilient, and courageous they are. Acknowledging strengths even when they fall short of meeting expectations shows your child that they still have a sense of worth despite not achieving the success they hope for.

The whole purpose of focusing on your child's strengths is to help them find reasons to believe in themselves. If you can convince them that they are worthy, by providing positive evidence, they can summon the courage to rise above the many hurdles they will experience at home, school, or in social groups.

Strategy 3: Explore Passions

There is just something magical about discovering a passion. It's like finding the missing piece of a puzzle and finally seeing the full picture.

One of the few times that you will see your child feeling good about themselves and focused for long periods of time on any task is when they are engaged in something they are passionate about. The joy they feel isn't solely based on finding something they are good at, but also the satisfaction of performing a task without the fear of failure and disappointment.

When exploring passions with your child, be mindful of your approach. Remember that you can only guide your child to discover interests they already have, not push them to love and adopt some of your interests. It may even be useful to think of this exercise not as "finding your child's passions" but instead as "creating opportunities for your child to find their passions on their own."

Therefore, your job as a parent will be to expose your daughter to as many different skills and activities as possible. Try not to select pleasurable skills and activities only, as this may not be where your child's passions lie. You may be surprised to learn that your child enjoys washing dishes, doing gardening jobs, or helping you prepare meals.

Observing your child's behavior will guide you on the kinds of interests and activities to expose them to. Notice what tasks they volunteer to do, or tasks that allow them to focus with ease (watching TV should not be one of them). At school, notice which subjects they often read and talk about. Purchase extra reading materials about the subject, or spend weekends doing creative projects based on the subject. The better you get at observing where and what your child naturally gravitates toward, the easier it will be to guide and support them with those interests.

For older kids, it may be difficult to observe interests because of the short amount of time you spend communicating and interacting with each other. The better approach would be to take your child out for lunch where you can bond and get to ask questions about their passions. Some of the questions you can ask include:

- What makes you smile?

- Which topic can you talk about for hours?

- Which people do you admire most in your life, and why?

- What school subject are you enjoying right now, and why?

- Describe a time when you felt proud of yourself. What were you doing?

- What is an activity that you have always wanted to try?

- What do you find easy to do?

- If you could choose to work any job, what job would you choose?

- What social causes do you support, and why?

- If you could change one thing about the world, what would it be?

These questions are supposed to be fun and informative. Your child should be the one doing most of the talking since they know what inspires them best. If there are any passions discovered during the conversation, schedule time to explore them deeper. Perhaps you can go along with your child to attend an art class, purchase a cookbook, enquire about joining a sports club, and so on.

The Value of Positive Self-Talk

It isn't uncommon for children with ADHD to speak negatively about themselves, especially when they are faced with unexpected challenges that trigger a sense of loss or failure. These might include challenges like being bullied at school, having trouble making friends, or experiencing some learning challenges.

The danger of negative self-talk, particularly during the early years of your child's life (the first eight years), is that it can mold beliefs about who they are, and what they are capable of (or in this case, incapable of).

For example, if it is ingrained in your child's mind that they aren't smart or can't process information, they may grow to have an unhealthy relationship with school. On a subconscious level, they anticipate having learning difficulties, which makes any attempt at learning feel punishing.

The opposite of negative self-talk—and perhaps just as influential on the mind—is positive self-talk. This is when your child speaks highly of themselves, and their abilities to succeed.

Positive self-talk shouldn't be confused with wishful thinking where your child believes in their potential. Instead, it should be seen as the awareness of positive qualities, behaviors, thoughts, and emotions that your child recognizes in themselves. In other words, positive self-talk is about highlighting the often downplayed positive aspects of who they are.

It's worth mentioning that your child may take longer to learn how to speak highly of themselves than the time it took to adopt negative beliefs. This has to do with the inherent negativity bias that exists in all human beings. By nature, our brains are wired to recall and have a stronger emotional reaction to negative information than positive information. Thus, to learn positive self-talk, your child will need to retrain their brain to recognize character strengths, small accomplishments, and opportunities for growth and improvement.

There are a few strategies that you can practice to help your child develop positive self-talk. These include:

1. Call out negative self-talk

Help your child recognize what negative self-talk sounds like by gently calling them out whenever they speak poorly of themselves. This can be as simple as saying, "That wasn't a kind way to speak about yourself." Some children may be blissfully unaware of how some phrases may be putting them down.

This is especially true when your child starts picking up on language spoken at school or in the media. It may also be good to use real-life scenarios to help them recognize negative self-talk, like pausing a show on TV and asking your child to weigh in on how a character speaks about themselves.

2. Create a safe space to talk about challenges

Make it a daily occurrence to ask your child how their day went. Ask questions about school, teachers, homework assignments, friends, and any other aspect of their life that may be a source of stress. Create a safe space where they can open up and share pleasant and unpleasant emotions. If there is something frustrating them, listen attentively and validate their feelings. The purpose of this is to help your child relieve stress so that they don't have to harbor negative feelings—or deal with their frustrations by blaming themselves.

3. Be fair with expectations

Naturally, children aim to please their parents. They will silently observe what behaviors get their parent's attention, and repeat them. When what you expect from your child is unrealistic, such as expecting high academic achievement from a child with learning disabilities, your child can feel disappointed in themselves when they can't fulfill those expectations. Plus, it might indirectly push them to get your attention in other ways, like misbehaving in class and throwing tantrums at home.

Being fair with your expectations starts by accepting your child for who they are. Get to understand how your child thinks, what motivates them, and which areas they excel in. Avoid comparing your child to the younger version of you, or other family members and friends. Praise them for the effort they make to be the best version of themselves.

4. Create a name for the inner critic

The inner critic is the voice that tells your child what they are incapable of. Your child may believe the lies spoken by the inner critic because it sounds like something they would say. Thus, it can be useful to separate the two voices that coexist—your child's authentic voice and the inner critic—by creating a separate name and identity for the inner critic.

This activity can be a lot of fun! On a sheet of paper, brainstorm attributes of the inner critic, such as their name, age, gender, favorite hobby, outlook on life, and a common negative belief. Try to make these attributes age-appropriate, so they can resonate with your child. Here is an example:

Name: Moaning Mona

Age: 7 years old

Gender: Female

Favorite hobby: Looking for things to complain about and feels upset when she doesn't get her way.

Outlook on life: Moaning Mona thinks that everything needs to go her way all the time. When this doesn't happen, she gets frustrated.

Common negative belief: "Nobody cares about me."

5. Help your child adapt

Positive self-talk is about having a fair and balanced view of yourself and others. In stressful situations, it can help you think of ways to adapt and find solutions to move forward. Whenever your child is faced with a problem, listen to what they have to share, then ask them what they are going to do about it. What are some of the immediate steps they can take to make the situation better, even if they can't solve the problem right now? An older child may be quick to provide a solution, whereas a younger child may need you to present three options and allow them to pick one.

For example, your child comes to you in tears about losing an important school assignment. You sit them down and listen to what they have to say. After hearing the story and validating their feelings, you ask them what they are going to do about it. Suddenly, the tears stop flowing and their logical brain switches on. After a minute, your child decides they will look inside their school bag and check the car to make sure it isn't somewhere around the house. You praise them for being an effective problem-solver and send them off to search for the missing assignment.

How to Use Positive Affirmations

Positive affirmations are a good example of positive self-talk. These empowering statements are designed to rewire the subconscious mind to think positively. When rehearsed on a regular basis, they can transform how one perceives themselves and the world around them.

If your daughter struggles with low self-esteem, consider encouraging them to create a daily practice of rehearsing positive affirmations. Doing this short but impactful exercise can enhance their moods and combat negative thinking. It also exposes them to positive language that they can use in everyday conversations with others. The best part though is that this exercise doesn't need your involvement. Below are examples of how your child can work with positive affirmations:

1. Reciting affirmations while looking at a mirror

Every morning, after brushing their teeth, encourage your child to take 5–10 minutes to recite positive affirmations while standing in front of their bathroom mirror. Remind them to look at themselves in the mirror, and even flash a smile or place a hand on their heart, as they go through the list of statements.

2. Use affirmation cards

Older girls might enjoy getting creative and creating their own affirmation cards. Below are the requirements to make them:

- Cut out standard 3-by-5-inch flashcards, and on each, write down a positive affirmation with a thick black marker.

- Use decorative craft supplies to make the face of the flashcards unique and appealing.

- Keep the pack of flashcards in an easily accessible place, like your bedroom.

When using affirmation cards, turn them face down, so the statements are hidden. Pick up random cards, turn them over, and read the positive affirmation out loud. Take a moment to reflect on the statement and significance of it.

3. Journaling

If your child can write and enjoys journaling, you can write down a few positive affirmations for them to unpack and interpret. This can be a fun way to encourage your child to think positively about themselves and remind them of their strengths whenever they are faced with tough challenges.

As a parent, you can also promote the use of positive language by being intentional about how you speak in the presence of your child. Be mindful of self-limiting phrases like "I can't do this" or "I never get it right." Your reactions to life events, particularly stressful events, show your child how to respond whenever they are faced with hard times.

List of Kid-Friendly Positive Affirmations

The most effective kind of positive affirmation is the one your child creates for themselves. However, before they do, they might want to get some inspiration and see how exactly positive affirmations are structured.

The basic structure of a positive affirmation is a sentence written in present tense and starting with "I." For example, a typical statement can start in the following ways:

- I am

- I love

- I deserve

- I believe

- I receive

The rest of the statement describes a positive experience that is currently happening or within reach. Here are a few examples using the introductions mentioned above:

- I am patient with myself.

- I love and accept myself.

- I deserve true friendships.

- I believe my goals are possible.

- I receive support from friends and family.

Below is a list of kid-friendly positive affirmations you can teach your child:

- I am special.

- I have a bright future ahead of me.

- I love what makes me unique.

- I deserve kindness.

- I am proud of who I am.

- I know better days are ahead of me.

- I believe in myself.

- I deserve to be listened to.

- I will achieve great things.

- I am a fighter who doesn't give up.

- I love my brain and body.

- I accept challenges that help me grow.

- I am capable of doing difficult things.

- I am grateful for my life.

- I am a positive influence on others.

- I am in control of my feelings.

Your child may not be the only one struggling with low self-esteem. As someone raising a girl with ADHD, you may have some doubts about your capabilities as a parent. Positive affirmations may be an effective tool to remind yourself that you are worthy of love and support, and that you are capable of raising a healthy and confident child.

Here are a few more positive affirmations specifically for you:

- I am a loving and capable parent.

- I know what is best for my child.

- I am willing to adapt to my child's needs.

- I deserve the love and support I give to others.

- I am doing my best and that is enough.

- I am allowed to pursue goals outside of my role as a parent.

- I deserve to enjoy the experience of parenthood.

- I am focused on progress, not perfection.

Chapter Takeaways

- Girls with ADHD tend to suffer from low self-esteem. Typical tendencies include adopting black-or-white thinking, or self-limiting beliefs as a result of acting differently from others.

- Social pressures also contribute to low self-esteem. Young girls are often expected to perform well academically, have good organizational skills, and concentrate on tasks. Not being able to fulfill these societal standards can negatively affect how girls see themselves.

- There are various ways that girls can boost their self-esteem and activate their inner girl power. Three of these strategies include challenging negative thinking, focusing on their strengths, and exploring passions.

- Parents can also encourage their children to speak more positively about themselves, through techniques like positive affirmations. Children don't need to be forced to stop thinking negatively; they just need to be taught and rewarded for using positive language, which will gradually transform their thinking patterns.

In the final chapter, you will find various exercises and prompts to help your child build a healthy self-esteem and confidence.

Chapter 7:

Navigating Friendships

If you go looking for a friend, you're going to find they're very scarce. If you go out to be a friend, you'll find them everywhere. –Zig Ziglar

How ADHD Affects Friendship Building

Friendships are an important part of your child's development. They can teach her important interpersonal skills, such as how to:

- take turns talking or playing.

- share belongings with others.

- work alongside others in a group.

- notice and respond appropriately to others' emotions.

- remember important information about others.

- follow social rules, like showing good manners.

As a result of the behavioral symptoms of ADHD that tend to make socializing difficult, your child may not be able to handle themselves confidently in social situations. For instance, their inattentiveness can make it harder to listen and reflect on what others are saying, or pick up on important social cues that inform the appropriate reactions.

However, having trouble socializing is not something irreversible. What may be difficult for your child to recognize is that the discomfort or awkwardness they feel during social interactions is not a reflection of them as a person, but rather a sign of poor social skills. This means they can get better at socializing and connecting with their peers—however, it will take a lot of practice!

Teenagers With ADHD and Friendship Shame

The inability to make friends can be particularly stressful for children with ADHD, but may struggle to make strong connections. A study found that 80% of children with ADHD experience negative peer relationships, and many of them don't have any mutual friendships (Rabiner, 2017).

This can cause identity issues since it is hard to make it through adolescence without having solid friendships. Part of the process of "coming of age" is developing a sense of belonging and finding your place in the world. Thus, when a child is unable to "fit in" and receive validation from their peers, it can negatively impact how they perceive themselves.

Like other teenage girls, those with ADHD tend to feel the pressure to define themselves by the strength of their friendships. When they grow up and realize that due to their condition, social interactions will be a lot harder, it can be enough to cause social anxiety or make them withdraw from others altogether.

Moreover, since there is a cultural expectation for girls to easily make friends, having a few or none can make girls with ADHD think they are incapable of being good friends. Of course, this is not true, and by learning the right social skills, they can come to this realization too.

There is no doubt that low self-esteem can also contribute to the difficulty in making and maintaining friendships. One way that this can manifest is through a phenomenon known as imposter syndrome. Imposter syndrome is a psychological experience where a person doubts their capabilities and believes that they are not who others think they are. As a result, they may avoid striving toward goals, celebrating accomplishments, or getting outside of their comfort zone because of the fear of being outed as fraud.

Teenage girls with ADHD may very well experience imposter syndrome, especially when they are given opportunities to socialize. The imposter inside of them might think: "If people get to learn who I really am, they will reject me." While rejection is an unavoidable part of relationships, it is not true that opening up to people leads to rejection.

The kinds of fears perpetuated by imposter syndrome can create unnecessary social challenges for teenagers, and in extreme cases, lead to self-sabotaging behaviors such as turning down invites, people-pleasing, succumbing to peer pressure, or deliberately rejecting others before they get rejected. It may also cause a sense of shame when the separation between friends is noticed, but feel hopeless about what to do to mend those relationships.

Friendship maintenance requires several skills, like verbal interplay, negotiation, empathy, good listening, and awareness of social cues and nonverbal body language. All of this can be a lot to remember at once, for a teenage girl with ADHD. In fact, even the thought of having to invest time and energy into checking up on friends, remembering birthdays, making time to go out, and still being available for emotional support is daunting.

The message that parents of children with ADHD should drive home is that sometimes, their children won't be able to meet the numerous expectations of the world. But failing to meet these expectations doesn't make them any less deserving of strong friendships. It simply means that they need to reframe what friendships mean to them and find ways of playing up their strengths, rather than apologizing or feeling ashamed of their limitations.

The following three sections will explore ADHD-friendly social strategies that you can teach your child at various ages. When going through these strategies, remember that your child may have unique ways of expressing who they are to the world. Create enough flexibility to help them put their own twists on these strategies, so they can step out as authentically as possible.

Social Strategies for Young Girls (Ages 3—8)

Social skills are not abilities that any child is born with. They must be learned and practiced over and over again, through age-appropriate strategies. As a parent of a young girl with ADHD, you may need to be more patient as your child learns how to communicate their needs and interact positively with others.

Below are three social strategies that you can teach them.

How to Be a Good Listener

Listening isn't just about keeping quiet when someone else is talking. It is also about being able to absorb information and make sense of it. Many social and communication skills rest on the ability to listen and respond appropriately to what is being said. Therefore, it is essential to help your child practice being a good listener from a young age.

Here are a few exercises to help your child practice listening:

- **Pause and reflect.** When reading a book to your child, stop after a few pages and ask them what they remember about the story thus far. If they leave out details, feel free to mention those, then summarize what you heard them say.

- **Freeze dance.** Put on some music in the living room and play a game of freeze dance. Get your child to dance while the music is playing and freeze when you randomly turn it off. The goal is to get them to become quicker at freezing as soon as the music stops.

- **Word chain.** Start by shouting out a random word that your child recognizes (i.e., they are able to read and write the word). Your child is required to listen to the word and shout out the next one, s*tarting with the last letter of the previous word.* In other words, if your word was "dog" then your child's word must start with the letter "g" such as "grass."

- **Create a fairytale.** Sit with your child and take turns creating a plot of a fairytale. Start with the lines, "Once upon a time there was…" then offer a sentence or two worth of detail. Your child will be challenged to listen to the information you provided and add details that would help the plot progress. Stop speaking whenever your child interrupts and ask them to pay attention.

- **Red light, green light.** This fun game teaches your child to listen and follow directions. Go outside to the backyard and have your child start at one end of the garden. When you say "Green light!" they are required to run as fast as they can, but stop immediately the moment you say "Red light!" To make the game more interesting for older kids, introduce new colors with different commands, like hopping on one leg, jumping like a frog, or doing jumping jacks.

How to Cooperate With Others

Cooperation is the ability to work together with other people to achieve mutual goals. As soon as your child starts kindergarten, they will need to learn how to get along with other children, play in groups, and even negotiate when tensions rise. Children who are cooperative may find it easier to participate and find their place in a classroom or community.

Here are a few exercises to help your child learn to be cooperative:

- **Work on activities as a family.** Find an activity that the whole family can get involved with. Maybe you are preparing a big dinner or looking to repaint and declutter the shed and can use some assistance from your family. Assign each person an age-appropriate task and give clear instructions on how to perform the job. Offer plenty of positive reinforcement and enforce the value of teamwork.

- **Play a board game.** Board games teach your child how to listen, follow instructions, and patiently wait their turn. Whenever your child breaks the rules, gently remind them of the process and why it is so important to follow. Model good sportsmanship by showing a positive attitude whether you lose or win.

- **Create a dance routine together.** Put on one of your child's favorites and follow along with your very own dance routine. If your child is too young to offer suggestions, take the lead and teach them basic movements, like clapping their hands, stepping to the side, shaking their hips, etc. Keep the routine between 30 seconds to a minute long, so your child can easily remember the steps.

- **Complete a puzzle.** Age-appropriate puzzles can teach your child how to work as a team, observe patterns, and solve problems. Since the activity involves a lot of trial and error, your child can practice healthy ways to cope with frustration.

How to Respect Personal Space

Children with ADHD are not always aware of physical boundaries, like respecting another person's personal space. For instance, your child might talk or sit very closely to someone, without realizing how uncomfortable it makes the other person feel.

Fortunately, there are several ways of teaching young kids about physical boundaries. Here are a few exercises to teach your child how to respect personal space:

- **Imaginary bubbles.** Teach your child that everyone has an imaginary bubble that they stand inside. To make people feel comfortable, we cannot enter their bubble, unless they invite us to (i.e., when they allow us to hug them). Your child can measure a person's bubble by standing an arm's length away from people they are talking to.

- **Carpet squares.** Cut out a carpet square big enough for your child to sit on. Whenever they are playing or eating, get them to sit on their carpet square. This will teach your child how much space they are allowed to occupy space and prevent them from invading other people's space.

- **Asking for permission.** Before your child leans over to kiss or hug someone, teach them to ask for permission. They might say, "Can I give you a hug?" or "Is it okay if I hold your hand?" Help your child anticipate "Nos" and approach them with a positive attitude.

Social Strategies for Pre-Teens (Ages 9—12)

When children reach pre-teenage years, socializing starts to become more sophisticated. They are expected to demonstrate social awareness, which is the ability to empathize and understand the perspectives of others. Unlike preschool, where selfishness can be overlooked, they are now encouraged to show some level of self-awareness and tolerance for others. As a parent, your task during these years will be to teach your daughter some level of emotional intelligence.

Below are three social strategies that you can start with.

How to Identify and Express Emotions

Teaching your child how to regulate their emotions can help them remain calm and in control during social interactions. What is important for them to understand at this age is that they won't always get their way, and when they don't, it isn't the end of the world. Another benefit of teaching your child how to identify and express emotions is that they can learn to recognize different emotions in others and respond with appropriate behaviors.

Here are a few exercises to help your child identify and express emotions:

- **Connect emotions to physical sensations.** Most of the time, emotions show up as physical sensations in the body, such as butterflies in the stomach, sweating, chest pain, or trouble breathing. Teach your child to pause and recognize what emotions their physical sensations might be alluding to. For instance, could their sudden headache be due to feeling stressed? Or is their chest tightness a result of feeling anxious?

- **Interpreting nonverbal cues to identify emotions in others.** Words may not always be used to express emotions. Sometimes, when words fail, people can display emotion through nonverbal communication. Teach your child to associate certain cues with specific emotions. For example, crying is a sign of sadness, laughter is a sign of joy, and avoiding eye contact is a sign of boredom.

- **Model the connection between emotions and behaviors.** Teaching your child emotional intelligence requires your participation. Use real-life positive or negative experiences as teachable moments to share what you are going through and the emotional impact it has on you. For example, when your child doesn't follow instructions, explain what thoughts and emotions come to your mind, and how that impacts you.

- **Recognize the role of environmental factors.** Besides psychological reasons, environmental factors can also affect your child's emotions. Whenever they are feeling off balance, ask your child to run through the checklist of physical needs: Are they tired? Hungry? Overstimulated? Or lacking connection? Encourage them to look for ways of responding to these needs, like taking a nap, grabbing a snack, spending time alone reading, or arranging a playdate with a friend or cousin.

How to Empathize With Others

Empathy can be taught from a very young age, but comes in handy when your child starts making friends and getting involved in sports or class projects. We can define empathy as the ability to place yourself in someone else's shoes and see the world from their perspective. Showing empathy builds confidence, increases tolerance of others, and reduces conflict and misunderstandings.

Here are a few ways to teach your child empathy:

- **Create empathy maps.** Take a big piece of cardboard paper and a few craft supplies. Ask your child to write down an emotion in big and bold letters, then around the emotion, brainstorm what others might think, say, or how they might behave when feeling that particular emotion.

- **Discuss current events.** Search online for current world events that are relevant and appropriate for your child to engage with. Print out articles or watch videos explaining these events, then discuss how the events might impact the environment, animals, children, parents, people working in specific industries, etc.

- **Encourage volunteer work.** Ask your child to pick a social cause they care about. Find a local group or community that assists with that specific cause, and sign your child up. For example, if your child cares about animals, visit a local animal shelter and ask how your child can get involved. Bear in mind, volunteer work can be an enriching activity the entire family can get involved with.

How to Negotiate With Others

It is important for your pre-teen to learn how to balance getting their needs met while being considerate of other people's needs too. It is unlikely that things will always go their way, especially when other people are involved. For instance, your child may not always agree with your parenting decisions or desire what their friends desire. Rather than shutting down or becoming emotional, you can teach your child how to find middle ground and strive for win-win situations.

Here are a few exercises to teach your child effective negotiation skills:

- **Introduce family meetings.** Once a month, schedule a family meeting where your child can participate in certain discussions related to the well-being of the family. You can bring up all sorts of topics during these meetings, such as recognition for good behaviors, concerning behaviors, upcoming family changes, or suggestions for new rules. Allow your child to voice their opinions and participate in decision-making.

- **Weigh the pros and cons.** Whenever your child pitches an idea, suggests a new family rule, or argues against certain consequences, encourage them to write a list of pros and cons related to the issue at hand. This will help them clarify their thought processes, balance logic and emotion, and give them an opportunity to look at the situation from different angles.

- **Avoid the winner vs. loser mindset.** Teach your child that negotiating is about finding common ground; things that they can agree on. Instead of trying to walk away as the winner, show them the benefit of bargaining and look for ways that both parties can walk away feeling satisfied with the outcomes. A question they can ask themselves is: *How can we both win?*

Social Strategies for Teens (Ages 13—17)

As mentioned earlier in the chapter, the ability to build and maintain social connections is vital for the well-being of teenagers. Not only does being socially active build healthy self-esteem, but it also offers teenagers a sense of belonging to a group, which is important for establishing identity. You can prepare your teenage girl for adult life by teaching them how to be a savvy communicator.

Below are three social strategies to help your child develop strong communication skills.

How to Strike Meaningful Conversations

By the time your child reaches adolescence, they are expected to know how to introduce themselves, strike conversations with people older and younger than them, and offer ideas or opinions to keep a conversation going. Being able to engage in meaningful conversations requires learning how to be a good conversationalist and express thoughts and emotions enthusiastically.

Here are a few exercises to teach your child how to strike meaningful conversations:

- **Know how to read a room.** Help your child develop situational awareness by learning how to behave in certain environments, and around certain people. Teach them what acceptable and unacceptable behaviors or conversations to have when speaking to adults versus their peers, or sitting at a library versus at a cafeteria. Practice looking at magazine photos with different contexts and asking your child to describe the unspoken social rules that those characters are expected to follow.

- **Practice sharing meaningful exchanges.** Use role-playing to come up with examples of real-life exchanges, like speaking to a cashier at a store, or being interviewed for a position at school. During the exchange, emphasize the importance of eye contact, asking relevant open-ended questions, and acknowledging or commenting on statements made by the other person.

- **Practice changing topics.** Help your child notice when a topic is phasing out and an opportunity for a new topic is created. For instance, when they notice boredom or disinterest (through nonverbal body language) they can either revive the current topic with an interesting question or think about a related topic to bring up that can add depth to the conversation. A great exercise to practice is getting your child to write down a general topic on a piece of paper and brainstorm several related topics that can keep a conversation going.

How to Be an Assertive Communicator

Teenagers who understand how to communicate assertively are able to stand up for themselves, express boundaries, and protect their interests and values, without being hurtful to others. This skill is especially important for teens since they are likely to encounter bullying and all sorts of peer pressure, and will need to be confident in advocating for their needs.

Here are a few exercises to practice assertive communication:

- **Different styles of communication.** Teach your child the four styles of communication: passive, aggressive, passive-aggressive, and assertive. Give examples of words and actions that reflect each style, and how each communicator would respond in different situations.

To further illustrate the differences, pick out a few video clips online that represent each style of communication and ask your child to look for clues that identify which style is being played out.

- **Help your child learn how to say "No."** Explain to your child that saying no keeps their mind and body safe and healthy. Support them whenever they set this kind of boundary over negotiable issues like what clothes they want to wear, receiving hugs from certain people, or expressing preferences to avoid certain foods.

- **The value of "I" statements.** Teach your child to express thoughts and feelings clearly and respectfully by using "I" statements. The simple formula to follow is: "I feel [insert emotion] whenever you [insert behavior]. I would like you to [insert reasonable request]." A completed statement might look like this: "I feel anxious whenever you rush me to complete a task. I would like you to allow me to have more flexibility in creating my homework schedule."

How to Use Text Messaging

A good portion of your child's social interactions won't happen face-to-face. Research shows that 61% of teenagers prefer texting their friends on messaging or video-chatting platforms, or interacting on social media instead of communicating in person (Loveland, 2018). Therefore, part of preparing your child to be an effective communicator is teaching them good texting etiquette.

Here are a few exercises to help your child stay safe and maintain good character while texting:

- **Create texting limits.** There are certain conversations that are more appropriate to have in person than online. For example, topics about personal traumas, politics, religion, or sexual orientation are better-explored face-to-face, where tone and intention can be understood. Explain to your child what topics they are not allowed to discuss, post, or share opinions about online.

- **Length of text rule.** A simple rule to decipher whether a conversation should be had over text or in person is this: If the message is longer than a paragraph or the voice note is longer than a minute, it is better to pick up the phone or set up a lunch date to engage in the conversation. Explain to your child how sending a long-winded text can be seen as inconsiderate of another person's time.

- **Put away phones when sitting with others.** Being on your phone in social settings can be seen as rude behavior. Encourage your child to put their phones away whenever they are around other people, and find ways to strike a meaningful conversation instead.

- **Practice kindness.** Explain to your child that what they post on social media or text to their friend or group chat can be held against them. The general rule to follow here is: If you wouldn't want to see your post or text message blown up on a billboard, don't send it. It is also important to teach your child that kindness extends to text messages too. Habits like gossiping or talking poorly of others are not acceptable.

Chapter Takeaways

- To build friendships, children must be able to listen, share, resolve conflict, follow rules, notice other people's feelings, and remember things that are important to other people. These behaviors don't come easy for children with ADHD.

- Girls with ADHD have a difficult time making friends. Young girls may have a lot of energy and find it hard to take turns, while older girls may miss social cues and feel left out in groups. For teens in particular, not being able to make friends can be hard since friendships are an important aspect of feeling a sense of belonging.

- Not only do parents have the opportunity to be their child's friend, but they can also teach them how to navigate friendships and be effective communicators.

Chapter 8:

Establish the Ground Rules

We are apt to forget that children watch examples better than they listen to preaching. –Roy L. Smith

Why Your Child Needs Rules

By now, you know how important it is to create a sense of structure and predictability in your child's life. The more organized and predictable your child's environment is, the more self-regulated they can be. One of the ways to create structure is to establish rules; these are clear expectations of behavior that serve as a reminder of how your child should relate to those around them.

The mention of rules might cause the average child to resist. However, rules provide more of a benefit to their well-being than your own. Living in a household with clear and supportive rules can help your child:

- Feel a sense of control over their actions, which can help manage their symptoms.

- Practice cooperating with the rest of the family and feel proud of their contribution to bringing harmony to the home.

- Build good habits that reinforce core life skills.

The older your child gets, the more you will need to step back as a parent. Stepping back isn't something you need to fear when you have built a structured environment for your child. For instance, even when you are not at home, they are able to follow set routines, manage their time wisely, organize their space, and carry out their assigned chores. All of this begins with creating the proper set of rules and holding the whole family accountable to them.

Where to Start With Creating Family Rules

Family rules are a set of values or statements that set a precedence on how family members should relate to one another. They can be based on a number of expectations, like showing respect to others, being helpful around the house, and cleaning up after yourself.

The purpose of creating them is to establish structure at home, introduce family rituals, and offer your child a standard when it comes to acceptable and unacceptable behaviors. But these rules are not just influential at home; they can also help your child listen and follow instructions outside the home too. Once you have set a standard of behavior for your child to follow, they are encouraged to continue the same habits in other places, like school or at a friend's house.

There are two things to remember when creating family rules: the first is to ensure they are realistic and practical. There is no point in creating standards when only two members of the family can comfortably follow them—you and your spouse. Your rules must be simple and age-appropriate so that even a young child who is still learning the difference between right and wrong behavior knows what is expected of them.

The second thing to remember is to enforce consequences for broken rules. What makes a child respect rules is knowing that there are consequences for not adhering to them. In a strange way, the presence of consequences creates an incentive for honoring the rules.

When establishing consequences, remember that the aim is to guide your child toward desirable behaviors, rather than punishing them for behaving badly. Consequences should be used as teachable moments that impart some kind of knowledge to your child, helping them make better decisions next time.

Now that you have a better understanding of the intent behind family rules, let's look at a few steps that will help you create them. Note that these steps apply to children of all ages. For teenagers, however, you can make an exception and allow them to help you brainstorm and identify some family rules.

Step 1: Consider Your Child's Age

In general, family rules apply to everyone. However, they are mindful of your children's ages. If you have more than one child, at different ages, then you will need to make sure the youngest and oldest children don't feel left out or unsupported.

Toddlers and preschoolers, for example, cannot remember a long list of rules. They can only memorize two to three rules that are simple and specific. Instead of a vague rule like "Treat others as you would like to be treated," you could tailor the rule to be more clear and specific, such as "No hurting others. Keep your hands to yourself" or "No yelling in the house. Speak with your soft voice."

Step 2: Consider the Behaviors You Want to Address

Every household struggles with certain behaviors. For instance, the children could be constantly fighting with each other, the house may look like a war zone most of the time due to toys and other stuff laying around, or maybe in your case—you are raising a child with inattentive ADHD who needs a lot of support to complete tasks. Based on what your current behavioral concerns are, you can create family rules that target those particular issues, and help the whole family learn healthier habits.

Step 3: Explain the Rules

Once you have a list of rules, call your family for a meeting and explain each rule to them. Offer real-life examples of how each rule can be practiced and when it would be broken. This may also be a good time to explain the consequences of breaking the family rules and emphasize once again the importance of following them.

A younger child may not be able to grasp the rule quickly. You may need to help them understand what each word means, like what "yelling" means, and what "yelling in the house" would look like. Later on, when your child yells, you can call their attention and help them recognize they are yelling, and yelling is not allowed inside the house.

You may need to repeat this over and over again until you believe they are aware of what is expected of them. Hanging up posters and charts around the house may also be good visual reminders of behaviors to follow.

Step 4: Enforce Consequences for Breaking Rules

It is important to stress that nobody is above the rule. What better way to reinforce this message than to create consequences for breaking rules? Once again, consequences are not a form of punishment, but rather a corrective measure to promote the desired behaviors.

For example, the consequence of yelling inside the house is losing 10 minutes of TV time. Taking away something desirable, like watching 30 minutes of TV, helps your child associate their yelling with something unpleasant. When a rule has been broken, respond immediately by issuing a consequence. This will save you from getting involved in power struggles or lecturing your child about their behavior.

The Three C's of Effective Discipline

Establishing ground rules is one of the most effective forms of discipline. However, it can be easy to get them wrong. Your approach to setting and enforcing rules determines how motivated your child is to follow them.

Below are three C's to effective discipline that every parent raising a child with ADHD needs to know. These three C's set the standard of what discipline should look like to get the best results from your child.

Clarity: Be Clear About Your Expectations

Children aren't generally known to be quick or intuitive thinkers. It takes a great deal of self-awareness before anyone (adults included) is able to figure out how to behave in certain contexts and situations. Therefore, as a parent, you cannot assume that your child knows what is acceptable and unacceptable behavior until you have explained the difference to them.

It can also help to have conversations about your expectations, in a calm and casual way. The best time, for example, would be during bath time, when both you and your little one are relaxed and can have an open discussion about rules. If you have an older child, try to get them outside of the house and have the conversation in a casual setting. Ideally, expectations and family rules should be a topic that comes up often because these are the standards that improve your family relationships.

Consistency: Be Consistent When Enforcing Behaviors

Have you ever found yourself disciplining your child for a specific undesirable behavior, then a few days down the line, giving them a pass for practicing the same undesirable behavior?

Hot and cold discipline can be confusing to a child with ADHD, especially a young child who desires structure and guidance. Even though they would prefer not to have rules at all, they at least expect the rules to be the same each day. In other words, they want to know that what was inappropriate yesterday will still be considered inappropriate today. As a way to test limits, your child will intentionally break rules. When they do this, their aim is to see how important it is to follow them. Will it result in a consequence? Or will mom and dad let it slide?

Discipline is more effective when rules are firm and "no" remains "no" regardless of the situation. As your child gets older, you can adjust the rules to provide more flexibility, but this too should be seen as a privilege that comes with age and good character.

Compassion: Show Compassion and Support When Correcting Behavior

The purpose of discipline is to guide your child toward desired behaviors. Thus, along the way, they will need encouragement to help them stay motivated. Catch your child when they are performing desirable behaviors, like cleaning up after themselves or remembering to pack their school lunch and offer positive reinforcement.

When a rule is broken, focus on criticizing their actions instead of them as a person, then issue a consequence and move on. Try not to dwell on the undesirable action after you have enforced a consequence. The truth is everyone makes mistakes sometimes, but what's important is that we can learn from them and do better next time.

Part of showing compassion is also creating consequences that match the behavior and aren't harsh or violent. You can measure how appropriate your consequences are by noticing how they impact your child. Observe your child's demeanor after a consequence has been issued. Do they look like they have received a wake-up call and are more mindful of following the family rules? Or do they seem withdrawn, scared, or disturbed?

Appropriate consequences drive the positive message of following rules, without damaging the relationship with your child. They give your child a newfound respect for rules because they have witnessed firsthand the cost of not sticking to them.

Age-Appropriate Discipline Tactics

We have discussed the importance of structure and establishing rules. But what about the day-to-day misbehaving, like whining or throwing tantrums, which don't necessarily break rules?

Naughtiness and pushing boundaries are examples of misbehavior that come with raising children. However, these behaviors aren't technically violations that warrant consequences, since they are common during a child's development.

For example, it is a known fact that young children may struggle to understand the word "No," and teenagers may have an attitude problem, and while these classify as bad behaviors, different discipline tactics apply.

Below is an age-by-age guide of alternative discipline tactics to use whenever your child is caught misbehaving:

Discipline Tactics for Young Girls Aged 3–8

Your young girl, aged 3–8, is constantly testing the waters to see what they can get away with. They have discovered that they are part of the world, rather than being a witness to it, and it is important to them to express their thoughts and emotions. Emotional meltdowns and power struggles are normal at this age until they learn self-regulation skills.

Another normal behavior is not quite grasping the concept of cause and effect. For example, your child may not understand why lying or cheating is wrong. You may need to explain several times the negative impact of bad behaviors and why it is better to avoid them. The type of discipline tactics that work best for this age group focuses on improving emotional regulation, controlling impulses, rehearsing desirable behaviors, and teaching empathy.

Here are a few tactics to practice with your child:

- **Reduce power struggles by offering options.** Instead of telling your little girl what to do, give them two choices of desirable behaviors. For example, you might say "Kelly, do you want to sit at the table and eat your lunch or clean up your toys?"

- **Ignore negative attention-seeking.** When your child is throwing a tantrum, distract yourself with another task around the house. Show an obvious disinterest in their unpleasant behavior, until they begin to calm down. Shift your attention back to your child and help them regulate their body through relaxation exercises like taking deep breaths, and loving physical touch.

- **Reinforce good behaviors through role play.** If you would like your child to perform certain tasks around the house, rehearse the desired behavior through role-playing. For example, you can pretend to be two cleaners hired to declutter a home, then go throughout the house looking for items to pick up.

- **Challenge bad behavior with empathy.** Whenever your child does something hurtful or causes an inconvenience for someone else, ask them how they would feel if it were done to them. This question gets your child to understand the impact of their behaviors by imagining if they were on the receiving end.

- **Identify and name feelings.** Help your child see the connection between emotions and behaviors by asking them to complete the following statement: I carried out [insert behavior] because I felt [insert emotion]. Next, help them think of better ways to cope with that strong emotion.

Discipline Tactics for Pre-Teens Aged 9–12

Your pre-teen, aged 9–12, is learning a lot about their identity, and where they fit in the world. They may be old enough to follow rules, but they have many questions about why certain behaviors are expected. For instance, you may find yourself having to explain basic principles, like why it is important to respect teachers.

The reason for all of this questioning is that your child seeks independence and feels a sense of control. They desire to live a life that feels "right" for them—not one that is dictated by their parents. You can expect a lot of pushback and power struggles, as your child swings between being cooperative to being difficult to guide. The kind of discipline tactics that work best for this age group are based on showing trust and giving your child autonomy while keeping them accountable for their actions.

Below are a few tactics to practice with your child:

- **Have open conversations about behavior.** Talk about problematic behaviors in open and respectable conversations. Leave all assumptions at the door, and ask questions to figure out what the problem might be and how to support your child. When approaching conversations, go with the intention to get to know your child better, and hopefully walk away having reached a mutual understanding.

- **Show respect to receive respect.** When your child reaches those pre-teen years, they begin to notice how you speak to them. Disrespectful, controlling, or condescending language can cause your child to shut down and stop listening. Treat your child with respect by watching your tone and choice of words. This will make it easier to get through to them.

- **Emphasize natural consequences.** Sometimes, the best teacher isn't a parent, but life itself. Natural consequences are those results that happen in response to your child's behavior. For example, the natural consequence of not studying for a test is getting a low grade. When your correction and guidance seem to not affect change in your child's behaviors, allow natural consequences to teach your child those valuable life lessons.

- **Don't appeal to your child's emotions.** During the pre-teen years, your child is going through several life and body changes. They may have frequent mood swings, which cause them to lose touch with reality. What they need is someone to be their anchor and offer some sense of structure and normalcy. Don't allow their emotions to cause you to be lenient on things that you are meant to be strict on. Keep your consequences black and white, so your child is reminded of what you expect from them.

Discipline Tactics for Teenagers Aged 13–17

Disciplining your teenager becomes a lot harder than when they were a young child or pre-teen. They see themselves as being grown up and having a mind of their own. At this stage of their life, they are more likely to be influenced by the behaviors you model in front of them than the long lectures you give. You may think that they are not watching what you do, but the truth is they are!

Your teenage child still needs guidance, but not in the traditional sense. Instead of setting the tone and pace for their life, they want you to walk behind them and be there to correct mistakes or offer support whenever they go astray. In other words, only intervene when you are asked to, or when it is necessary.

Below are a few discipline tactics to practice with your child:

- **Teach your child problem-solving skills.** Whenever your child misbehaves or lands themselves in hot water, don't rush to provide solutions. Stay calm and ask them what they think should happen. Say, "What are you going to do about this?" or "How do you plan on solving this problem?" Support them in their decisions, and follow up to see how they are coping.

- **Be open to negotiate.** The next stage of life after adolescence is adulthood. Therefore, during this stage, you want to teach your child effective negotiating skills, which will come in handy as an adult. For instance, when you disagree on expectations, such as what time to make curfew, listen to their argument and see whether you can reach a compromise. Praise them for their ability to negotiate and present win-win situations.

- **Hold your child accountable for bad behavior.** Stay consistent in correcting bad behavior, even when it seems like your child doesn't care or the consequence isn't working. Your consistency in issuing appropriate consequences for bad behavior is what eventually makes it too costly and undesirable.

- **Avoid taking away important events.** While it is okay to withhold certain privileges when issuing consequences, there are some that carry a sentimental value that shouldn't be taken away, such as singing practice (if your child is passionate about singing) or prohibiting them from attending prom. Taking away these privileges won't improve your child's behavior or teach them any valuable life lessons. It will only make them bitter and rob them of meaningful experiences.

What's important to remember about disciplining children with ADHD is that the everyday demands of life are a struggle for them. This means that they are more likely to have behavioral issues than non-ADHD children. Be patient when correcting inappropriate behaviors, and try not to lose sight of the many positive things they do right.

Chapter Takeaways

- Children with ADHD need a structured and predictable environment to help them self-regulate and practice healthy social behaviors.

- One of the best ways to create this type of environment is to establish family rules, which are a set of expectations that govern acceptable and unacceptable behaviors.

- When establishing rules, remember to consider your child's age, any problematic behaviors you can target, and appropriate consequences for breaking the rules.

- Your child is more likely to respect rules when they follow the three C's of effective discipline: clear, consistent, and compassionate. Be clear about what you expect, enforce desirable behaviors consistently, and be compassionate when correcting bad behavior.

Chapter 9:

A Positive Approach to

Parenting

Behind every young child who believes in himself is a parent who believed first. –Matthew Jacobsen

Why Parenting Style Matters When Raising a Girl With ADHD

The symptoms of ADHD can be difficult for both children and parents to cope with. Research has found that parents raising children with ADHD are more likely to experience increased parental stress (Modesto-Lowe et al., 2008). One of the biggest challenges for parents is learning how to adapt their parenting approach to accommodate their child's needs.

The traditional style of parenting is strict and authoritarian and places an emphasis on obedience, rather than learning and responding to the child's needs. This approach doesn't work when raising neurodivergent children, such as girls with inattentive ADHD.

In the 1990s, a gradual shift away from authoritarian parenting toward permissive parenting began. The upside to this was that parents were now more responsive to the needs of their children; however, they were unable to create structure and appropriate boundaries for their children to follow. Instead of the "my way or the highway" style of parenting, parents were now saying, "absolutely anything for you, my angel!"

Both these approaches—authoritarian and permissive parenting—are ineffective in providing the kind of nurturing and supportive environment for your child. While one is more warm and responsive than the other, they do not provide enough guidance and discipline.

The better approach, which combines both styles of parenting, is the authoritative approach. With this style, parents are empathetic toward their children but are still able to set expectations for them to follow and hold them accountable for improper behaviors.

Authoritative parenting does away with forms of punishment or seeking to assert dominance over children. Instead of parents leading from the front or the back, they walk alongside their children and play the role of mentor in their lives.

As a result, children are encouraged to be children and make mistakes, which their parents encourage them to learn from. Being able to explore and fail helps children build self-awareness and learn how to reflect on their own behaviors. Studies have shown that children with ADHD, who are raised by authoritative parents, are more likely to display self-control, and independence, and perform better in academic and social environments (Wexelblatt, 2020).

Taking a New Approach to Parenting: The Four Golden Rules

The good news about parenting styles is that they can be easily adjusted. You don't need to have any previous exposure to authoritative parenting to practice it. However, you must be willing to rethink how you relate to your child and the various ways you respond to their cognitive, social, and emotional needs.

Below are four golden rules to remember when adopting the authoritative style of parenting:

Rule 1: Practice Self-Control

Get into the habit of checking in with yourself and assessing how you are doing. Ask yourself: What are some of my physical, mental, and emotional needs that require urgent attention? And what will I do to respond to those needs?

Authoritative parenting is about creating a safe and nurturing environment for your child to thrive. But how can this happen when you are feeling overwhelmed or anxious?

You must have control over your own emotions in order to model calm and mindful behavior. Make time for yourself during the day, even if it means taking an hour to spend alone. If you are struggling with health or psychological issues, consider seeking professional help, so you can learn how to manage your symptoms.

Rule 2: Adjust Your Mindset

Your mindset is the set of beliefs that influence how you experience the world. These beliefs cover all areas of your life, including your approach to parenting. What many parents don't realize is that their parenting mindset is significantly influenced by inherited beliefs from childhood, such as "children are meant to be seen, not heard" or "good girls don't cry."

It is therefore important to reflect on some of these beliefs and assess the role they play in your parenting approach. On a piece of paper, write down the beliefs that come to mind when you think of children, or how they ought to be raised. Perhaps some of these beliefs came from your parents, and others from society. Identify beliefs that may reinforce authoritarian or permissive parenting, then reframe them to represent authoritative parenting.

For example, you may have grown up believing that "Children are expected to do well at school," or on the other side of the spectrum, "Children don't need to do well at school." These beliefs reflect authoritarian and permissive parenting respectively. If you wanted to adjust your mindset and reframe those beliefs to reflect authoritative parenting, the new belief would be something like "Children do well at school when they are motivated to."

You may also need to adjust the perceptions you hold about your child. Instead of seeing a limited child, you may choose to see a child with limitations. Or when thinking about how differently your child's life path may look to other children, choose to focus on the areas where their strengths shine through, rather than magnifying the areas where their weaknesses are more apparent.

Your mindset shapes the kind of child you see, and how you choose to raise them. As Dr. Stuart Shanker said, in his book *Self-Reg*, "See a child differently, and you see a different child" (Shanker & Barker, 2016).

Rule 3: Seek Emotional Support

Parenting a child with ADHD can be lonely when you are doing it alone, or without a solid support system. Collaborate with your significant other, if both parents are still involved in your child's life, or seek emotional support from close friends, family members, ADHD support groups for families, and even schoolteachers.

There is an African proverb that says: It takes a village to raise a child. This is certainly true when you are raising a child with special needs, who may need more guidance and support as they grow.

Rule 4: Be Present and Stay Consistent

A distinct characteristic of authoritative parenting is being emotionally available for your child. This means being in touch with your own feelings, so you can sustain a close bond with your child. When they are expressing thoughts and emotions, for example, you should be able to hold space for them, validate their experiences (even when you can't relate), and provide reassurance.

It is also important to remain consistent in how you relate with your child. If possible, make sure that your reactions, moods, and discipline approaches remain consistent. Avoid sudden emotional outbursts or approving behaviors you disapproved of yesterday. Your child should be able to predict how you are going to respond to certain situations, whether good or bad.

When you decide to adjust your parenting approach, your child will be understandably suspicious. Give them time to process the new strategies. They may not respond favorably to your actions and discipline immediately, but eventually, when they see your consistency, they will learn to respect the new approach.

If your child is old enough to understand, you can explain the new approaches to them. For instance, when trying out a new form of discipline, you can say "We are going to try something new that will help you calm down. Are you comfortable trying it with me?"

Shifting to Positive Parenting

Under the umbrella of authoritative parenting is a specific style known as positive parenting. Research has found that positive parenting can reduce the intensity of behavioral challenges in children with ADHD, as well as set clear expectations and build their self-esteem (Hoath & Sanders, 2002).

Positive parenting encourages praise and positive attention to reinforce good behavior and help children adopt a growth mindset. The aim is to catch children behaving in desirable ways, rather than giving them attention only when they are misbehaving. This shift has the ability to minimize problematic behaviors and provide more incentives to behave well.

Another key feature of positive parenting is to stay calm and avoid overreacting to your child's undesirable behaviors. When you are stressed and frustrated, your child learns to associate relationships with behaviors like yelling, criticizing, or controlling. But when you are calm and are able to teach your child self-soothing techniques (e.g., deep breathing, counting to 10, leaving the room, etc), they are able to learn how to manage their emotions and have a more positive outlook on relationships—they can associate relationships with care, respect, and support.

5 Positive Tips for Raising Happy Girls

There are critiques about positive parenting, specifically when it comes to discipline. Some parents believe that providing children with positive attention creates unclear limits or expectations. It is important to distinguish between positive parenting and permissive parenting, since these two approaches may look similar.

Positive parenting seeks to raise well-adjusted children by emphasizing responsiveness over-reactivity. When a child is crying, for example, the positive parenting approach would be to help them calm down, validate their emotions (e.g., "I know you really want to play outside"), then create a boundary or enforce a consequence (if the parent is correcting bad behavior).

On the other hand, permissive parenting seeks to appease the child. When a child is crying, the permissive approach would be to give them what they want to avoid conflict. While permissive parents do attempt to create boundaries, they have trouble following through with them. This style of parenting falls high in affection and responsiveness but low in the discipline.

If you would like to practice positive parenting, here are five tips to help you get started:

1. Empathize with your child

The next time you think, "Why on earth would they do that?" take a moment to pause and get inside your child's head. Try to imagine yourself as a five or 12-year-old and the views you would have about the world. Recognize that your child makes choices according to their level of perception and understanding. This is why they may not always know when they are behaving inappropriately. Empathizing with your child can help you learn more about their needs, fears, and desires, as well as the best ways to support them.

2. Distract your child from the behaviors you don't like

This strategy works for toddlers and young children. Instead of saying, "Don't do that!" draw your child's attention to something else. Providing an alternative activity helps your child focus on good behaviors that earn them positive attention. Within seconds, they have forgotten about picking out grandma's beautiful plants from the garden and now enjoy the praise of helping collect fallen leaves. Are they aware that picking out grandma's plants was wrong? No, but they don't need that kind of negative attention either.

3. Use humor and playfulness to incentivize good behaviors

Acting silly and making jokes can correct bad behavior without creating tension. For example, if your child has walked into the house with muddy feet, you can make a joke about the dog leaving paw prints. Thereafter, make a game out of cleaning up the dirt on the floor and praise your child when they have completed the cleanup. For older children, particularly teenagers, create challenges/competitions that come with sweet rewards. For example, if they can keep their room clean for a week, then you can take them out for a movie on the weekend.

4. Keep your interactions mostly positive

According to researcher and psychologist, John Gottman, stable and happy relationships maintain a 5:1 ratio when it comes to positive and negative interactions. For every negative feeling or interaction, there must be five positive feelings or interactions that follow (Benson, 2017). Seek to maintain this ratio with your child by having more positive encounters than negative ones. This could mean deciding on which inappropriate behaviors are worth calling out, and which ones you can brush off.

5. Find ways to say "Yes"

This tip shouldn't be confused with being permissive. Finding ways to say "Yes" is about avoiding being dismissive of your child's needs, and instead finding acceptable (parent-approved) alternatives. In other words, they cannot get what they want, but they can find another way to achieve their goal. For example, you may not want your teenager going out late at night with their friends, but you may be comfortable with your child inviting their friends and throwing a party at your place. Or maybe you refuse to buy your little girl cookies at the store, but make a deal to bake fresh cookies over the weekend.

The key to positive parenting is to not take good behavior for granted, and to make all efforts to catch your child when they are behaving in desirable ways. They will certainly make mistakes and forget the rules you taught them—and when this happens, they will have no choice but to face the consequences. But your focus on good behaviors helps them develop self-regulation skills and stay motivated to do better next time.

Chapter Takeaways

- Parenting styles describe the philosophies and strategies used to raise children.

- The traditional authoritarian "my way or the highway" style of parenting places an emphasis on obedience and enforces punishment for not following rules. For a girl child with ADHD who may not follow instructions or gets distracted easily, this style of parenting can be overwhelming.

- Permissive parenting, on the other hand, is high on responsiveness but low on discipline, which means that a child is free to do whatever they please—a recipe for disaster when raising a child with ADHD.

- Studies have shown that authoritative parenting, a blend of both authoritative and permissive parenting, can help address behavioral challenges in children with ADHD.

- With authoritative parenting, your child is encouraged to explore the world and make mistakes, while having you by their side as a source of wisdom and guidance.

- Positive parenting, a form of authoritative parenting, is a newer approach to raising children, which has also been found to work wonders on children with ADHD. The aim of positive parenting is to encourage desirable behaviors by paying attention to what your child is doing right and increasing the number of positive interactions between you.

In the final chapter, you will find various positive parenting exercises to practice!

Chapter 10:

Exercises and Journal Prompts

To become really good at anything, you have to practice and repeat, practice and repeat, until the technique becomes intuitive. –Paulo Coelho.

Emotional Regulation Exercises and Prompts

Emotional regulation is the ability to exert control over your emotions and choose better-coping behaviors during stressful situations. Below are a few exercises and prompts to help your child manage their emotions.

Describing Emotions

Suitable age group: 3–8 years old

Instructions: Go through the table below and choose the appropriate emotions to answer the questions.

Angry	Fearful	Happy	Love	Sad	Shame
Irritated	Scared	Joyful	Cared for	Hurt	Shy
Grumpy	Worried	Glad	Kindness	Neglected	Self-conscious
Frustrated	Panicked	Hopeful	Sympathetic	Disappointed	Embarrassed
Annoyed	Nervous	Relieved	Affectionate	Lonely	Humiliated
Furious	Overwhelmed	Excited	Liking	Rejected	Guilty

1. How do you feel when you are told you can't play outside?

_____

_____

2. How do you feel when another child doesn't want to share their toys?

_____

_____

3. How do you feel when you meet someone new for the first time?

_____

_____

4. How do you feel when you get a big hug from your pet?

_____

_____

5. How do you feel when you don't have anyone to play with?

_____

_____

6. How do you feel when you face consequences for bad behaviors?

_____

_____

7. How do you feel when you are eating your favorite food?

_____

_____

8. How do you feel when someone says, "Well done!"

_____

_____

9. How do you feel when someone says, "NO!"

_____

_____

10. How do you feel when your family spends time together?

_____

_____

Opposite Action

Suitable age group: 9–12 years old

Instructions: Think about times when you felt the urge to act impulsively. Perhaps you wanted to slam the door behind you, say a curse word, throw an object, or hide away from everyone. Now, imagine you did the opposite action. What might that look like?

Complete the table below to identify the opposite action for common urges. The first two rows have been filled out for you.

When I feel...	I want to...	The opposite action would be...
Scared	Hide away from everyone	Share what I am feeling with my parents so they can help me.
Angry	Yell at whoever made me angry	Go to a quiet room and take a few deep breaths until I feel calm.
Scared		
Angry		
Embarrassed		
Sad		

When I feel...	I want to...	The opposite action would be...
Shame		
Lonely		
Rejected		
Dismissed/not listened to		
Controlled		
Criticized		

Check the Facts

Suitable age group: 13–17 years old

Instructions: Emotions don't always match what is happening in reality. For example, you might feel embarrassed to talk to a group of friends because you think they will judge you. But is this really true? Or have your fears gotten the best of you?

Think about a situation that you feel strongly about. For example, you might feel angry toward your parents, sad about not doing well at school, or embarrassed because of being easily distracted. Answer the following questions to check whether your feelings match what is happening in reality.

1. Describe the situation that you feel strongly about.

2. Could there be another way of looking at the situation? Write down two other interpretations.

3. Are you assuming the worst-case scenario? How so?

4. Are your feelings based on opinion or facts? How so?

5. If the worst was to happen, how would you cope? What actions would you take to make yourself feel better?

6. If someone you care about was in the same situation, what advice would you give them?

Accumulate Positive Experiences

Suitable age group: All

Instructions: When you are feeling overwhelmed, shift your attention away from the negative thoughts and do something positive! Find healthy distractions around the house that can help you regain a sense of calm and control.

For the next 30 days, challenge yourself to practice at least one healthy distraction from the table below. Check off activities as soon as you complete them.

Plant seeds in the garden	Clean your room	Take a walk	Play dress up
Read a chapter	Create a dance routine	Ride a bike	Complete a crossword

from a book			puzzle
Go swimming	Make your favorite meal	Make a hair appointment at the salon	Think about a pleasant memory
Call a friend	Watch a movie	Take a blanket outside and stargaze	Take a selfie
Play with your pet	Draw something	Create a vision board	Write a "thank you" letter
Practice a musical instrument	Go to a party	Visit the zoo	Play a board game
Take a nap	Visit the local library	Go bowling	Wear your favorite outfit
Have a picnic in the garden	Do a random act of kindness	Take a relaxing bubble bath	Conduct a science experiment

Self-Esteem and Confidence Exercises and Prompts

It is normal to go through periods where you doubt yourself. However, when these negative thoughts start to consume your life and make you feel less than everyone else, it is time to do something about them. The following exercises and prompts will help your child start the journey of developing healthy confidence and self-esteem.

Get to Know Me

Suitable age group: 3–8 years old

Instructions: Answer the following prompts to help others get to know you better.

1. My name is…

_____

_____

2. My favorite color is…

_____

_____

3. My friends think I am special because…

_____

_____

4. My mom says I am good at...

_____

_____

5. One thing that I love about myself is...

_____

_____

6. Something that makes me feel happy is...

_____

_____

7. I matter the most to...

_____

_____

8. An activity I really enjoy is...

_____

_____

9. My future dream is to...

_____

_____

10. I am passionate about…

_____

_____

What Makes a Good Friend?

Suitable age group: 9—12 years old

Instructions: Making good friends is like baking cupcakes. You need to have the right ingredients in a bowl to create a delicious masterpiece! Can you think of the ingredients that make a good friend?

List five traits that make a good friend. Describe what each trait looks like (try to give practical examples) and why it matters to you.

Here's an example:

Trait	Honesty
What does it look like?	Telling me the truth and being open about their feelings.
Why does it matter?	A friend who is honest can give me good advice whenever I need help or support.

Fill in the following tables with your five traits.

Trait #1	
What does it look like?	
Why does it matter?	

Trait #2	
What does it look like?	
Why does it matter?	

Trait #3	
What does it look like?	

Why does it matter?	

Trait #4	
What does it look like?	
Why does it matter?	

Trait #5	
What does it look like?	
Why does it matter?	

Daily Self-Esteem Journal

Suitable age group: 9–17 years old

Instructions: For the next seven days, take 10 minutes to journal about positive outcomes for the day. Think about the things you are grateful for, what you were able to accomplish (remember, progress over perfection), and any other positive experience that made your day feel pleasant.

Monday Prompts

1. One thing that made me smile today...

_____

_____

2. Something interesting I watched...

_____

_____

3. I am proud of myself for...

_____

_____

Tuesday Prompts

1. I am grateful for (think of someone)...

_____

2. Something I found fun today was...

3. A small victory I achieved...

Wednesday Prompts

1. Today was unique because...

2. A personal strength I displayed...

3. Something new I learned...

Thursday Prompts

1. A good habit I practiced today was...

_____

_____

2. A positive belief that kept me going...

_____

_____

3. I helped someone else by...

_____

_____

Friday Prompts

1. Something kind I did toward myself...

_____

_____

2. Today I challenged myself by...

_____

_____

3. I felt positive when…

_____

_____

Saturday Prompts

1. Something motivational I listened to…

_____

_____

2. A relaxing activity I did…

_____

_____

3. Someone who made my day was…

_____

_____

Sunday Prompts

1. A beautiful thing I noticed about myself…

_____

_____

2. One word to describe my life right now...

_____

_____

3. Something that made me feel good today...

_____

_____

Gratitude Letter

Suitable age group: 13–17 years old

Instructions: On the line space provided, write a letter to someone who has helped you build confidence over the years. This should be a person who regularly offered encouragement, and advice on how to solve problems, and showed up when you were feeling down. In your letter, mention all the small and big ways they have made a positive difference in your life. You can decide whether to share this letter with the special individual, or not.

_____

_____

_____

_____

_____

_____

_____

_____

_____

_____

_____

_____

Getting to the Root of Self-Esteem

Suitable age group: 13–17 years old

Instructions: If you want to discover what a healthy self-esteem does and doesn't look like, you can simply think back to moments when you displayed natural confidence and felt proud of who you are, or alternatively think back to times when you were at your lowest.

Answer the following questions to travel back to the past and discover what causes your confidence to peak and drop.

1. Think back to the past and recall a moment when you felt confident about yourself. What was happening?

_____

_____

_____

_____

2. What emotions do you recall feeling at the time? Write them down.

_____

_____

_____

_____

3. What kinds of thoughts and beliefs were you having? E.g., "I love my life."

_____

_____

_____

_____

4. Next, think back to a time when you were full of self-doubt and felt bad about yourself. What was happening?

_____

_____

_____

_____

5. What emotions do you recall feeling at the time? Write them down.

_____

_____

_____

_____

6. What kinds of thoughts and beliefs were you having? E.g., "I'm not good enough."

_____

_____

_____

_____

7. Now that you are aware of what you think and feel when your confidence peaks and drops, write down a few positive statements you can rehearse when you notice your confidence lowering. E.g., "I am a fighter, and I will overcome this situation."

_____

_____

_____

_____

8. What positive distractions can you turn to, wherever you seek to minimize negative thinking? E.g., Journaling

_____

_____

_____

_____

_____

_____

_____

Positive Parenting Exercises and Prompts

Positive parenting is a gentle approach to raising well-adjusted and confident children. Below are a few exercises and prompts to help you practice positive parenting techniques.

Daily Positive Parenting Checklist

Positive parenting isn't only practiced when disciplining your child; it can also be practiced in daily interactions. Below is a checklist that you can go through each day, reminding you to offer your child positive attention.

Behaviors	Yes/No	Comments
Pay a genuine compliment.		
Praise your child's efforts.		
Validate your child's feelings.		
Maintain the 5:1 positive interaction ratio.		
Give your child a warm hug.		
Affirm your love with phrases like "I love you."		
Ignore negative attention-seeking behavior.		

Behaviors	Yes/No	Comments
Show your child respect by listening, maintaining eye contact, and speaking with a kind tone of voice.		
Spend quality time with your child.		

Positive Communication

Like any parent, you can get frustrated with your child sometimes. During those moments, it is normal to speak negatively. Positive parenting is all about finding the good, even in terrible situations. As such, your challenge is to find helpful—instead of hurtful—ways to speak about your child's bad behaviors.

Complete the following table by providing positive alternatives for these common phrases. The first two rows have been completed for you.

Instead of saying...	You can say...
"She never keeps quiet"	"She is talkative"
"My child is lazy"	"My child needs reminders to complete chores"

Instead of saying…	You can say…
"She asks a lot of questions"	
"My child makes me tired"	
"She doesn't listen"	
"She is stubborn"	
"My child has behavioral issues"	
"She has strange interests and ideas"	
"She is different from other children"	
"My child can't do basic things"	
"I am worried about my child"	

Establishing the Right Consequences

Are you feeling a bit unsure about issuing consequences? This is normal. Many parents fear creating consequences that are either too rigid and stifling or too lenient and counterintuitive. The following exercise will help you see how natural consequences come into effect, and the lessons your child can learn from them.

Behavior	Consequence	Lesson Learned
E.g., Your child forgets to hand in the homework assignment.	Your child gets a zero for the assignment.	Your child learns to be more organized next time.
E.g., Your child calls their friend a harmful word.		
Your child decides to study the day before the exam.		
Your child forgets sports uniform at home.		
Your child leaves their dirty laundry on their		

Behavior	Consequence	Lesson Learned
bedroom floor.		
Your teenager constantly wakes up late for school.		

Helping Your Child Take Responsibility

Whenever your child is misbehaving, you have an opportunity to guide them toward desirable behavior. By doing this, you are helping them correct their mistakes and take responsibility for their actions.

One way to guide your child is by using "Think starters" instead of "Think stoppers" whenever you are correcting your child's behavior. For example, instead of saying "You are making a noise!" you can say "I can't hear the other person on the phone. May you please use your soft voice?"

Fill out the following table to practice identifying think stoppers and using think starters instead.

Situation	Think Stoppers	Think Starters
E.g., You are on a Zoom meeting and your child is making noise in the background.	"You are making too much noise."	"I can't hear my colleagues. May you please use your soft voice?"

Situation	Think Stoppers	Think Starters
You want your child to help clean up the kitchen.		
One child is upsetting another.		
You are out at the mall and your child is whining.		
Your child forgot to pack her backpack the night before school.		
Your child is frustrated about completing a task and says, "I can't do this."		
Your child is afraid of making friends.		

Conclusion

I think that the best thing we can do for our children is to allow them to do things for themselves, allow them to be strong, allow them to experience life on their own terms... let them be better people, let them believe more in themselves. —Joy Bell C

Raising a daughter with ADHD can be a unique experience. For one, many doctors overlook the symptoms of their condition because, well, ADHD is still considered a "boy's disorder." Not only that, but society seems to be holding on to those old stereotypes about how a girl is supposed to behave, which makes pinning ADHD very difficult.

For most of your child's life, she has grown up feeling different from others. She doesn't seem to be sociable like other girls or cope with the demands of school. Her condition has isolated her, making her doubt who she is capable of becoming.

The good news is that it doesn't have to be this way. Your daughter is diagnosed with ADHD—not some incurable disease. Yes, certainly, their development won't look identical to that of non-ADHD children, or boys with ADHD for that matter, but she is still capable of building cognitive, social, and behavioral skills—albeit at a slower pace.

This guide was specifically designed to turn "Can'ts" into "Cans" so instead of reading about your daughter's limitations, you can explore all of the possibilities related to raising a child with ADHD.

Throughout the chapters, we have gone in-depth, looking at how you can help your child manage some of the common symptoms of inattentive ADHD. The takeaway message is that your child's symptoms can be managed, and they can be taught desirable social behaviors, with just a little bit more TLC and guidance.

My hope is that you are also inspired to adopt the positive parenting style, an approach to parenting that has been found beneficial for children with ADHD. The trick with positive parenting is to praise your child when you see them trying, and seek to build their self-esteem with positive emotions and language.

You are the best person to guide your daughter through this journey of childhood and adolescence. You understand what their emotional needs are and how to create a safe environment where they can thrive. Your wisdom, patience, and positive attention are exactly what they need to feel comfortable exploring the world, learn the difference between acceptable and unacceptable behavior, and discover who they can be!

So, continue doing your best. Every small effort you make counts.

If you have enjoyed reading through this guide, please leave a review by scanning the QR code below. A review is not just a means to gain exposure; it is a powerful way to assist others in discovering this book and finding support for their parenting challenges. By sharing your thoughts and experiences, you contribute to a growing community of individuals seeking guidance and understanding. Your review can play a vital role in connecting those in need with valuable resources, making a positive impact on their parenting journey. So, please consider leaving a review not only to enhance visibility but also to empower and uplift fellow parents, enabling them to navigate their struggles with greater ease and confidence.

About the Author

Richard Bass is a well-established author with extensive knowledge and background on children's disabilities. Richard has also experienced first-hand many children and teens who deal with depression and anxiety. He enjoys researching techniques and ideas to better serve students, as well as providing guidance to parents on how to understand and lead their children to success.

Richard wants to share his experience, research, and practices through his writing, as it has proven successful for many parents and students.

Richard feels there is a need for parents and others around the child to fully understand the disability or the mental health of the child. He hopes that with his writing people will be more understanding of children going through these issues.

Richard Bass has been in education for over a decade and holds a bachelor's and master's degree in education as well as several certifications including Special Education K-12, and Educational Administration.

Whenever Richard is not working, reading, or writing he likes to travel with his family to learn about different cultures as well as get ideas from all around about the upbringing of children, especially those with disabilities. Richard also researches and learns about different educational systems around the world.

Richard participates in several online groups where parents, educators, doctors, and psychologists share their success with children with disabilities. Richard is in the process of growing a Facebook group where further discussion about his books and techniques could take place. Apart from online groups, he has also attended training regarding the upbringing of students with disabilities and has also led training in this area.

A Message from the Author

If you enjoyed the book and are interested on further updates or just a place to share your thoughts with other readers or myself, please join my Facebook group by scanning below!

If you would be interested on receiving a FREE Planner for kids PDF version, by signing up you will also receive exclusive notifications to when new content is released and will be able to receive it at a promotional price. Scan below to sign up!

Scan below to check out my content on You Tube and learn more about Neurodiversity!

References

Aburdene Derhally, L. (2016, March 23). *How (and why) to create emotional safety for our kids.* Washington Post. https://www.washingtonpost.com/news/parenting/wp/2016/03/23/how-and-why-to-create-emotional-safety-for-our-kids/

Ackerman, C. E. (2017, May 23). *18 Best self-esteem worksheets and activities (incl. PDF).* PositivePsychology.com. https://positivepsychology.com/self-esteem-worksheets/#kids-self-esteem

ADHD Editorial Board. (2021, December 13). *The messy student's guide to organization.* ADDitude; ADDitude. https://www.additudemag.com/helping-adhd-students-get-organized-for-school/

ADHD Editorial Board. (2022, April 18). *What is ADD? Inattentive ADHD explained.* ADDitude; New Hope Media LLC. https://www.additudemag.com/slideshows/symptoms-of-inattentive-adhd/

Ali, Z. (2019, January 2). *ADHD in girls: Symptoms, early warning signs, and complications.* Www.medicalnewstoday.com. https://www.medicalnewstoday.com/articles/315009#conditions-with-similar-symptoms

Beck, C. (2021, May 3). *Self-monitoring strategies for kids.* The OT Toolbox. https://www.theottoolbox.com/self-monitoring-strategies-for-kids/

Beheshti, A., Chavanon, M.-L., & Christiansen, H. (2020). *Emotion dysregulation in adults with attention deficit hyperactivity disorder: a meta-analysis.* BMC Psychiatry, 20. https://doi.org/10.1186/s12888-020-2442-7

Benson, K. (2017, October 4). *The magic relationship ratio, according to science.* The Gottman Institute; The Gottman Institute. https://www.gottman.com/blog/the-magic-relationship-ratio-according-science/

Bhatt, A. (2022, August 19). *120 Daydreaming quotes and sayings for daydreamers.* The Random Vibez. https://www.therandomvibez.com/daydreaming-quotes-day-dreamers/

Brown, T. E. (2022, September 20). *7 Truths about ADHD and intense emotions.* ADDitude. https://www.additudemag.com/adhd-emotional-regulation-video/

Buzzanko, C. (2020, May 22). *The key to ADHD emotional regulation? Cultivating gratitude, pride and compassion.* ADDitude. https://www.additudemag.com/emotional-regulation-adhd-kids-strategies/

CDC. (2020, March 24). *Family rules.* Www.cdc.gov. https://www.cdc.gov/parents/essentials/structure/rules.html

CDC. (2021, September 23). *Data and statistics about ADHD.* Centers for Disease Control and Prevention. https://www.cdc.gov/ncbddd/adhd/data.html

Cherry, K. (2022, October 23). *Positive reinforcement and operant conditioning.* Verywell Mind; Verywellmind. https://www.verywellmind.com/what-is-positive-reinforcement-2795412

Child Mind Institute. (2021, August 19). *Helping girls with ADHD make friends.* Child Mind Institute. https://childmind.org/article/helping-girls-with-adhd-make-friends/#:~:text=Girls%20with%20ADHD%20can%20have

Connolly, M. (2022, November 21). *ADHD in girls and women: Symptoms and treatment for ADD in females.* ADDitude. https://www.additudemag.com/adhd-in-girls-women/

Coste, B. (n.d.). *Parenting quotes on discipline: On loving unconditionally.* Www.positive-Parenting-Ally.com. https://www.positive-parenting-ally.com/quotes-on-discipline.html

Crowe, A. (2022, June 20). *27 Positive affirmations for kids that boost self-esteem.* Www.prodigygame.com. https://www.prodigygame.com/main-en/blog/positive-affirmations-for-kids/#:~:text=Positive%20affirmations%20for%20kids%20about%20self%2Desteem&text=I%20am%20important%20and%20special

Day, N. (2021, November 1). *How to teach your child to identify their strengths - boost self esteem*. Raising an Extraordinary Person. https://hes-extraordinary.com/child-strengths-list-tips

Dewar, G. (2018, July 2). *Positive parenting tips: Getting better results with humor, empathy, and diplomacy*. Parenting Science. https://parentingscience.com/positive-parenting-tips/

Evans, C. (2013). *Making sense of assessment feedback in higher education*. Review of Educational Research, 83(1), 70–120. https://doi.org/10.3102/0034654312474350

Frank, M., & Solden, S. (2021, December 13). *Low self-esteem in ADHD women: Emotional and psychological help*. Www.additudemag.com. https://www.additudemag.com/low-self-esteem-adhd-women/#:~:text=As%20a%20result

Frye, D. (2020, November 6). *Children with ADHD avoid failure and punishment more than others, study says*. ADDitude. https://www.additudemag.com/children-with-adhd-avoid-failure-punishment/

Frye, D. (2022, May 10). *Criticism from parents may worsen ADHD symptoms in children*. Www.additudemag.com. https://www.additudemag.com/parental-criticism-may-worsen-adhd-symptoms/

Furukawa, E., Alsop, B., Sowerby, P., Jensen, S., & Tripp, G. (2016). Evidence for increased behavioral control by punishment in children with attention-deficit hyperactivity disorder. *Journal of Child Psychology and*

Psychiatry, 58(3), 248–257. https://doi.org/10.1111/jcpp.12635

Gilmore, H. (2014, December 13). *Help for the daydreaming child.* Psych Central. https://psychcentral.com/pro/child-therapist/2014/12/helping-the-daydreaming-child#4

Goldberg, D., & Rief, S. (2023, January 7). *Be on time! Get organized with ADHD time management and routines.* ADDitude. https://www.additudemag.com/time-management-skills-organization-help-adhd/

Gordon, S. (2022, January 26). *5 Tips for teaching kids to engage in positive self-talk.* Verywell Family. https://www.verywellfamily.com/how-to-teach-kids-to-engage-in-positive-self-talk-5205084

Hamaker, S. (2015, October 30). *8 Reasons to encourage your child's daydreaming.* Crosswalk.com. https://www.crosswalk.com/family/parenting/kids/8-reasons-to-encourage-your-child-s-daydreaming.html

Hoath, F. E., & Sanders, M. R. (2002). A feasibility study of enhanced group triple P — Positive parenting program for parents of children with attention-deficit/hyperactivity disorder. *Behaviour Change,* 19(4), 191–206. https://doi.org/10.1375/bech.19.4.191

Jackson, C. (2022, June 5). *ADHD and time management in children: Tips on how to practice.* Www.joonapp.io. https://www.joonapp.io/post/adhd-time-management

Jaksa, P. (n.d.). *The disorganized child: Strategies for helping children with ADHD stay focused.* Www.addcenters.com. https://www.addcenters.com/articles/the-disorganized-child-strategies-for-helping-children-with-adhd-stay-focused

Jennifer. (2021, August 25). *25 Basic house rules for families and how to create your own.* The Intentional Mom. https://www.theintentionalmom.com/family-house-rules-free-printable/

Jones, H. (2022, January 17). *Do ADHD symptoms differ in boys and girls?* Verywell Health. https://www.verywellhealth.com/do-adhd-symptoms-differ-in-boys-and-girls-5207995

Kash, N. (2022, July 20). *Maladaptive daydreaming vs. Inattentive ADHD: Comparing symptoms, treatments.* ADDitude. https://www.additudemag.com/maladaptive-daydreaming-vs-inattentive-adhd/

5 Keys to parenting ADHD. (2021, September 7). Kids Empowered 4 Life. https://kidsempowered4life.com/5-keys-to-parenting-adhd/

Lakhotia, P. (2021, February 5). *Positive self-talk for kids: Importance and 12 ways to teach it.* MomJunction. https://www.momjunction.com/articles/positive-self-talk-for-kids-examples-importance_00708881/

Lampert, L. (2021, December 21). *A parent's guide to age-appropriate discipline.* Parents. https://www.parents.com/toddlers-preschoolers/discipline/tips/smart-discipline-for-every-age/

Liew, M. (2020, February 18). *11 Signs of overly-critical parents and how to handle them.* Life Advancer. https://www.lifeadvancer.com/signs-of-overly-critical-parents/

Linehan, M. M. (2015). *DBT skills training handouts and worksheets, second edition.* https://mydoctor.kaiserpermanente.org/ncal/Images/Emotion%20Regulation%20DBT%20Skills%20ADA%2004292020_tcm75-1598999.pdf

Littman, E. (2021, January 25). *How to make friends as an adult: A guide for women with ADHD.* ADDitude. https://www.additudemag.com/how-to-make-friends-adult-woman/

Louick, R. (2022a, September 19). *5 Key steps for raising assertive kids.* Big Life Journal. https://biglifejournal.com/blogs/blog/how-to-raise-assertive-child

Louick, R. (2022b, October 1). *7 Tips to give effective feedback to your child.* Big Life Journal. https://biglifejournal.com/blogs/blog/give-effective-feedback-child

Loveland, M. (2018, September 12). *Teens would rather text and chat online with their friends than hang out in real life, study says.* Insider. https://www.insider.com/study-teens-would-rather-text-with-friends-than-hang-out-in-real-life-2018-9

Lovering, N. (2022, May 18). *ADHD and emotions: Relationship and tips to manage.* Healthline.

https://www.healthline.com/health/adhd/emotional-regulation

Low, K. (2022, April 19). *Children with ADHD need structure in their lives to stay focused.* Verywell Mind. https://www.verywellmind.com/why-is-structure-important-for-kids-with-adhd-20747

Lumiere Children's Therapy. (2019, August 14). *Let's talk: How to help your child engage in meaningful conversations.* Lumiere Children's Therapy. https://www.lumierechild.com/lumiere-childrens-therapy/2019/8/14/lets-talk-how-to-help-your-child-engage-in-meaningful-conversations

M, K. (2022, December 12). *101 Inspirational parenting quotes that reflect love and care.* MomJunction. https://www.momjunction.com/articles/amazing-quotes-on-parenting-to-inspire-you_00104303/

MacKay, J. (2019, December 16). *50 Inspirational (and actionable) time management quotes.* RescueTime Blog. https://blog.rescuetime.com/time-management-quotes/

Martin, B. (2016, May 17). *The 5 C's of effective discipline: Setting rules for children.* Psych Central. https://psychcentral.com/lib/the-5-cs-of-effective-discipline-setting-rules-for-children#1

Modesto-Lowe, V., Danforth, J. S., & Brooks, D. (2008). ADHD: Does parenting style matter? *Clinical Pediatrics, 47*(9), 865–872. https://doi.org/10.1177/0009922808319963

Morin, A. (2022a, September 2). *Positive reinforcement to improve a child's behavior.* Verywell Family; Verywellfamily. https://www.verywellfamily.com/positive-reinforcement-child-behavior-1094889

Morin, A. (2022b, September 21). *7 Social skills you can start teaching your child now.* Verywell Family. https://www.verywellfamily.com/seven-social-skills-for-kids-4589865#toc-respecting-personal-space

Musser, E. D., Karalunas, S. L., Dieckmann, N., Peris, T. S., & Nigg, J. T. (2016). Attention-deficit/hyperactivity disorder developmental trajectories related to parental expressed emotion. *Journal of Abnormal Psychology*, 125(2), 182–195. https://doi.org/10.1037/abn0000097

O'Donnell, J. (2020, May 13). *10 Cell phone etiquette tips to teach your tween.* Verywell Family. https://www.verywellfamily.com/texting-and-cell-phone-etiquette-for-tweens-3288602

Playful Notes. (2017, January 28). *12 Inspiring positive parenting quotes that will warm your heart.* Playful Notes. https://playfulnotes.com/positive-parenting-quotes/

Pragmatic Parent. (2018, November 26). *7 Ways to help kids identify feelings and control emotions.* The Pragmatic Parent. https://www.thepragmaticparent.com/help-kids-identify-control-emotions/

Qualls, M. (2021, March 31). *4 Things to know about emotional safety.* First Things First. https://firstthings.org/4-things-to-know-about-emotional-safety/

Rabiner, D. (2017, March 22). *Helping teens with ADHD develop friendships.* ADD Resource Center. https://www.addrc.org/helping-teens-with-adhd-develop-friendships/

Raising Children. (2022, September 15). *Friendships: Children and pre-teens with attention deficit hyperactivity disorder (ADHD).* Raising Children Network. https://raisingchildren.net.au/school-age/development/adhd/friendships-children-pre-teens-adhd

Rebbapragada, S. (2022, November 29). *100+ Best and cute quotes about friendship for kids.* MomJunction. https://www.momjunction.com/articles/best-funny-quotes-about-friendship-for-kids_00680631/

Richie. (2022, September 9). *100 Beautiful self confidence quotes for girls and teens.* Homeschool and Humor. https://www.homeschoolandhumor.com/self-confidence-quotes-for-girls-and-teens/#:~:text=%E2%80%9CYour%20self%2Dconfidence%20is%20not

Roychoudhury, R. (2021, March 22). *100 Best practice quotes to make perfect.* Kidadl.com. https://kidadl.com/quotes/best-practice-quotes-to-make-perfect

Shanker, S., & Barker, T. (2016). *Self-reg: how to help your child (and you) break the stress cycle and successfully engage with life.* Penguin Press.

Silva Casabianca, S. (2021, May 6). *15 Cognitive distortions to blame for your negative thinking.* Psych Central. https://psychcentral.com/lib/cognitive-distortions-negative-thinking

Sturm Niz, E. (2020, July 7). *Why and how to teach your kids mindfulness.* Parents. https://www.parents.com/health/healthy-happy-kids/why-and-how-to-teach-kids-mindfulness/

University of Washington. (2006). *Family tools module 2: Promoting positive parenting.* https://depts.washington.edu/dbpeds/FamilyiTools(PositiveParenting).pdf

Veal, C. (2021, February 24). *How to help your kid when they regularly misread social signals with friends.* Caroline Maguire. https://carolinemaguireauthor.com/help-your-kid-with-social-signals/

Watson, S. (2021, June 14). *Teens and tweens: ADHD and time-management skills.* WebMD. https://www.webmd.com/add-adhd/childhood-adhd/teens-tweens-adhd-time-management#:~:text=Eliminate%20Dawdling

Wexelblatt, R. (2020, June 28). *In defense of authoritative (not authoritarian!) parenting.* ADDitude. https://www.additudemag.com/authoritative-parenting-discipline-adhd-kids/

Wonderopolis. (n.d.). *Do you daydream?* Www.wonderopolis.org. https://www.wonderopolis.org/wonder/do-you-daydream/

Zhang, J. (2020, December 28). *65 ADHD quotes to help you understand it better.* Emoovio. https://emoovio.com/adhd-quotes/

Image References

Cameron, J. M. (2020). *Photo of girl writing on white paper [Online image].* In Pexels. https://www.pexels.com/photo/photo-of-girl-writing-on-white-paper-4143794/

Cottonbro Studio. (n.d.). *Smiling girl sticking her head out of a playhouse window [Online image].* In Pexels. https://www.pexels.com/photo/smiling-girl-sticking-her-head-out-of-a-playhouse-window-5789953/

Cottonbro Studio. (2020). *A girl in red sweater holding her phone while talking to her friend [Online image].* In Pexels. https://www.pexels.com/photo/a-girl-in-red-sweater-holding-her-phone-while-talking-to-her-friend-6214560/

Fairytale, E. (2020). *Two women smiling at each other [Online image].* In Pexels. https://www.pexels.com/photo/two-women-smiling-at-each-other-3893732/

Fring, G. (2021). *Photograph of a child covering her ears while sitting on a sofa [Online image].* In Pexels. https://www.pexels.com/photo/photograph-of-a-child-covering-her-ears-while-sitting-on-a-sofa-7447257/

Grabowska, K. (2020a). *Mother comforting crying daughter [Online image]*. In Pexels. https://www.pexels.com/photo/mother-comforting-crying-daughter-6134926/

Grabowska, K. (2020b). *Mother looking at her daughter [Online image]*. In Pexels. https://www.pexels.com/photo/mother-looking-at-her-daughter-6255537/

Grabowska, K. (2021). *A mother getting upset to her daughter [Online image]*. In Pexels. https://www.pexels.com/photo/a-mother-getting-upset-to-her-daughter-6957249/

Holmes, K. (2020). *Crop kids doing homework together [Online image]*. In Pexels. https://www.pexels.com/photo/crop-kids-doing-homework-together-5905841/

Karpovich, V. (2020). *Woman in yellow floral dress carrying baby girl over the shoulder [Online image]*. In Pexels. https://www.pexels.com/photo/woman-in-yellow-floral-dress-carrying-baby-girl-over-the-shoulder-4617297/

Lach, R. (2021). *Mother and daughter drawing together [Online image]*. In Pexels. https://www.pexels.com/photo/mother-and-daughter-drawing-together-9872953/

Li, E. (2021). *Smiling ethnic girl telling secret to best friend [Online image]*. In Pexels. https://www.pexels.com/photo/smiling-ethnic-girl-telling-secret-to-best-friend-7169009/

Mart Production. (2021). *Woman in white shirt sitting on bed [Online image]*. In Pexels. https://www.pexels.com/photo/woman-in-white-shirt-sitting-on-bed-8472873/

Monstera. (2021). *Black mother with daughter drinking water from glasses [Online image]*. In Pexels. https://www.pexels.com/photo/black-mother-with-daughter-drinking-water-from-glasses-7114373/

Nilov, M. (2021). *A girl reading a book [Online image]*. In Pexels. https://www.pexels.com/photo/a-girl-reading-a-book-8923561/

Piacquadio, A. (2020). *Sad isolated young woman looking away through fence with hope [Online image]*. In Pexels. https://www.pexels.com/photo/sad-isolated-young-woman-looking-away-through-fence-with-hope-3808803/

Podrez, A. (2021). *A woman and a girl praying with eyes closed [Online image]*. In Pexels. https://www.pexels.com/photo/a-woman-and-a-girl-praying-with-eyes-closed-6951489/

Shuraeva, A. (2021a). *A mother hugging her daughter [Online image]*. In Pexels. https://www.pexels.com/photo/a-mother-hugging-her-daughter-7204167/

Shuraeva, A. (2021b). *Girl wearing sunglasses sitting on womans lap [Online image]*. In Pexels. https://www.pexels.com/photo/girl-wearing-sunglasses-sitting-on-woman-s-lap-8083658/

Summer, L. (2021). *Sad woman sitting in room [Online image]*. In
Pexels.   https://www.pexels.com/photo/sad-woman-
sitting-in-room-6382662/

Wormwood, M. (2021). *Photograph of a girl using a cell phone while
sitting with her mother [Online image]*. In Pexels.
https://www.pexels.com/photo/photograph-of-a-girl-
using-a-cell-phone-while-sitting-with-her-mother-
7484416/